125 BEST
Cheesecake
RECIPES

125 BEST
Cheesecake
RECIPES

GEORGE GEARY

125 Best Cheesecake Recipes
Text copyright © 2002 George Geary
Photographs copyright © 2002 Robert Rose Inc.

For complete cataloguing information, see page 186.

Disclaimer
The recipes in this book have been carefully tested by our kitchen and our tasters. To the best of our knowledge, they are safe and nutritious for ordinary use and users. For those people with food or other allergies, or who have special food requirements or health issues, please read the suggested contents of each recipe carefully and determine whether or not they may create a problem for you. All recipes are used at the risk of the consumer.

We cannot be responsible for any hazards, loss or damage that may occur as a result of any recipe use.

For those with special needs, allergies, requirements or health problems, in the event of any doubt, please contact your medical adviser prior to the use of any recipe.

Design & Production: PageWave Graphics Inc.
Editor: Carol Sherman
Copy Editor: Launie Lapp
Recipe Testing: Jennifer MacKenzie
Photography: Mark T. Shapiro
Food Stylist: Kate Bush
Props Stylist: Charlene Erricson
Color Scans: Colour Technologies

Cover image: Fresh Raspberry Hazelnut Cheesecake (page 107)

We acknowledge the financial support of the Government of Canada through the Book Publishing Industry Development Program (BPIDP) for our publishing activities.

Published by: Robert Rose Inc.
120 Eglinton Ave. E., Suite 800, Toronto, Ontario, Canada M4P 1E2
Tel: (416) 322-6552   Fax: (416) 322-6936

Printed and bound in Canada by Canadian Printco Limited
4 5 6 7 8 9 10   CPL   09 08 07 06

To my Mom
I love you more than you will ever know.

Acknowledgments

INSPIRATION FOR THIS book came from so many people. Thank you Dad for teaching me to do my very best, and Mom for being my biggest fan. Monica and Patti, you are the best sisters a brother could ever have. Thank you Neil for eating never-ending plates of cheesecakes, letting me know when they needed fixing and when I got them exactly right. Jonathan, you keep my computer in top shape and are always there to help at a moment's notice. Teri, you wear so many hats — media coach, newsletter editor, tour guide assistant — I thank you for them all. Thanks Arlene Ward for giving me the push to write about my best subject. Lisa Ekus, who's not just my agent, but my friend. Driscoll's Berries, for believing in me as much as I believe in "The Finest Berries in the World." Susan, Mark, Lori, Quinn and Karyn, thank you. Sylvia and Lorene at the Los Angeles County Fair, where I received my first blue ribbon for cheesecake years ago. Cathy and the entire staff at Central Market Cooking Schools. You are the best!

Karen Tripson, thank you for all of your insight and direction from proposal to manuscript. Carol Sherman for guiding this new author. Bob Dees at Robert Rose for helping me realize this dream. Jennifer MacKenzie for testing and re-testing the recipes until they were perfect. PageWave Graphics for making this book so beautiful. Thanks especially to the thousands of students I have enjoyed teaching over the years to make the perfect cheesecake.

Contents

Introduction

YOU WILL FIND cheesecakes on restaurant menus from New Jersey to Toronto. Everybody loves them. Simple, yet elegant, cheesecakes are much easier to make than other traditional cakes, such as a layer cake, for instance, but equally, if not more, impressive.

Once when I was having a holiday dinner party my mom was helping me cut my Blue Ribbon Cheesecake. She tasted a little piece and exclaimed, "Oh you can't serve this" with a look on her face as if she had eaten a cheesecake made with salt instead of sugar. What in the world did I do wrong, I thought? And what will I serve now? But then she said, "Nobody will appreciate this cheesecake, so I'll just have to take it home." You have to watch mom. She could eat a whole cheesecake by herself in one day. In fact, come to think of it, maybe she has. I hope the 125 cheesecake recipes presented here will inspire such exciting results for you.

Tools and Equipment to Make Perfect Cheesecakes

THE FIRST STEP in creating a perfect cheesecake every time is having the proper tools. The wrong-size pan or poor-quality tools will cause problems that are not easy to solve. Many of the tools that you'll need will have other uses in your kitchen and last a long time, so it's worth purchasing quality equipment the first time. You'll never have to replace it.

HAND TOOLS
Rubber spatulas

A rubber spatula is the perfect tool for scraping a bowl clean. It also allows for the most thorough mixing of ingredients, the least waste of ingredients when turning them into the baking pan and an easy cleanup. The new silicone spatulas, which are heatproof to 600°F (300°C), are ultra efficient because they can go from the mixing bowl to the stovetop. Commercial-quality spatulas are more flexible and durable than grocery-store brands.

Balloon whisk

To achieve perfectly beaten egg whites or whipped cream use a sturdy whisk. They come in many sizes for different jobs. If you buy only one whisk, select a medium-size one.

Liquid measuring cups

The most accurate way to measure liquid ingredients is with a glass or Pyrex® measuring cup with a pouring spout. They are widely available in sizes ranging from 1 cup (250 mL) to 8 cups (2 L). Place the measure on a flat surface and add the liquid until it reaches the desired level. When checking for accuracy, bend over so that your eye is level with the measure. Pyrex® cups can also be used in the microwave to melt butter and heat water.

Dry measuring cups

The most accurate way to measure dry ingredients is with metal nesting measuring cups. They usually come in sets of four to six cups in sizes ranging from ¼ cup (50 mL) to 1 cup (250 mL). Spoon the dry ingredient into the appropriate cup and then level off by sliding the flat end of a knife or spatula across the top of the cup. The exceptions are brown sugar and shortening, which need to be packed firmly in the cup for correct measurement.

Measuring spoons

The most accurate measuring spoons are metal. A set of sturdy spoons ranging from ⅛ tsp (0.5 mL) to 1 tbsp (15 mL) is necessary for measuring small amounts of both liquid and dry ingredients.

Mixing bowls

A nested set of small, medium and large mixing bowls will be used countless times. Having the right size bowl for the job, whether it's beating an egg white or whipping a quart (1 L) of cream, helps the cooking process. Ceramic, glass and stainless steel all have their merits, but I think stainless steel is the most versatile.

Microplane® zester/grater

A Microplane® zester/grater with a handle is the best tool for quickly removing zest from lemons or other citrus fruits. To use, rub the Microplane® over the skin so you can see the zest. Do not zest any of the white pith, as it has a bitter taste. It is also good for grating hard cheeses and chocolate.

Garlic press

A garlic press is the fastest way to turn a clove of garlic into small bits. This method has a stronger flavor through the release of oils than garlic sliced with a knife.

BAKING PANS

Invest in quality pans; they conduct heat more efficiently, so cooking is more even and the desired results are achieved on top and bottom.

Have an assortment of baking pans on hand for the most flexibility in making a variety of cheesecakes. But if your storage is limited or you are frugal, you can get by with one 9-inch (23 cm) cheesecake pan with 3-inch (7.5 cm) sides and one 13-by 9-inch (3 L) metal baking pan with 2-inch (5 cm) sides, which can also serve as a water bath pan.

CHEESECAKE PANS VERSUS SPRINGFORM PANS

I recommend using a good-quality cheesecake pan instead of a springform pan for several reasons. A cheesecake pan has solid sides with a pop-up bottom — a flat metal disc similar to a tart pan bottom. The sides do not have a spring that can rust and the pan does not need to be greased. (See Sources, page 185, for sources of quality baking pans.)

A springform pan, on the other hand, needs to be replaced after only a few uses because the sides buckle and the spring in the release stops working. The bottom must fit very tightly in the pan edge or it leaks. As well, the pan bottom has a zigzag texture and a lip that make it hard to unmold the cheesecake. When using a springform pan, lightly grease the pan or cut a circle of bleached parchment paper for the bottom. I would also make a band of parchment for the sides of the pan. Avoid using unbleached parchment paper as it will brown your cheesecake, making it look too dark.

In addition to the pans mentioned above, a good selection would include:
- 6-inch (15 cm) cheesecake pan with 3-inch (7.5 cm) sides
- 10-inch (25 cm) cheesecake pan with 3-inch (7.5 cm) sides
- jellyroll pan or half-sheet pan
- 12-cup muffin tin

BAKING INSTRUCTIONS FOR DIFFERENT-SIZE PANS

If you have different-size pans than the ones recommended, you can still make the recipes in this book by following the instructions below:

A good rule of thumb: If you are using a $2\frac{1}{2}$-inch (6 cm) deep pan instead of a 3-inch (7.5 cm) deep pan, increase the diameter of the pan size called for in the recipe by 1 inch (2.5 cm). Bake about 5 to 10 minutes less than what the recipe specifies. For example: In place of the 9-inch (23 cm) pans with 3-inch (7.5 cm) sides, substitute a 10-inch (25 cm) springform pan with $2\frac{1}{2}$-inch (6 cm) sides. The cheesecake will not be as deep.

DECORATING TOOLS

Pastry bag and tip

A pastry bag allows you to pipe beautiful garnishes and decorations to make perfect-looking cheesecakes. They can also be used for cookies, appetizers, mashed potatoes and more. Pastry bags come in a variety of materials, so choose one that's easy to wash.

Offset spatula

This tool has a long handle and a flexible metal blade that is set at an angle. It's ideal for smoothing out batters in pans without dragging your knuckles through the mixture and is great for spreading icing over cheese-cakes. Offset spatulas come in a variety of lengths and thickness. Choose one that feels comfortable in your hand.

ELECTRIC EQUIPMENT
Stand mixer
Tough jobs such as beating cream cheese and sugar require the power of a stand mixer. Select one that's sturdy and comes with a rounded bowl and whip and paddle attachments. Professional quality is not essential, but a 6-quart KitchenAid® is a delight to use and takes care of any mixing needs.

Hand-held mixer
A hand-held mixer is great for small jobs. It allows easy access around the bowl when beating egg whites and whipping cream. It also makes it easier to mix ingredients in hot pots that are still on the stove.

Food processor
Select a sturdy processor large enough to handle the volume of the recipes you use most often. My 14-cup Cuisinart® has worked well for me over many years.

Common Ingredients

CHEESE
Regular versus lower-fat cheese
There is a big difference between regular and lower-fat cheese. For the best results when baking cheesecakes, use regular or full-fat cheese only. The process of removing fat from cheese reduces the flavor and texture. Lower-fat and non-fat cheese do not melt properly, and sometimes not at all, when baked or heated. Substituting a lower-fat cheese in a standard cheesecake recipe diminishes the final product. Save the lower-fat cheese for use in cold dips, spreads and sandwiches.

The Guilt-Free chapter, however, contains cheesecake recipes that are an exception to the regular-cheese-only rule. They are specially formulated to compensate for the different fat and moisture contents of reduced-fat cheese, allowing you to experience the best results with the fewest calories.

Storing fresh and ripened cheese
The cheeses used in this book can typically be categorized as fresh cheese and ripened cheese.

Fresh cheese is usually soft and needs to be wrapped tightly in plastic wrap, placed in an airtight container and stored in the coldest part of the refrigerator. If any mold develops, it's time to toss the cheese out.

Ripened cheese is typically firm or semi-firm and should be wrapped in waxed paper and stored in the warmest section of the refrigerator. Storing the cheese in its original wrapping inside a resealable bag will prevent the cheese from assuming the odors of other things in the refrigerator. If any mold develops on the surface, there's no harm done; just slice it off before using.

Cream cheese

Cream cheese is a fresh cheese made from cow's milk and by law must contain 33% milk fat and no more than 55% moisture to be classified as such. When buying cream cheese, select name brands only. Some of the store brands have added sorbic gum acids and moisture, which diminish the texture of cheesecake.

Neufchâtel cheese is a reduced-fat cream cheese that contains 23% milk fat, which means a few less calories.

Light or lower-fat cream cheese has about half the calories of regular cream cheese. Whipped cream cheese, which is soft because it has air whipped into it, has slightly fewer calories. Non-fat cream cheese, of course, has no calories from fat and is best used on a bagel or sandwich, not for baking cheesecake.

REGIONAL CHEESE
Adding extra richness and body

Cottage cheese is a fresh cow's-milk cheese that comes in small, medium and large curds with various fat contents. The moisture content is high. The creamed style has extra cream added and extra calories as a result. Cottage cheese is drained to become other styles of cheese, of which the driest version is farmer's cheese.

Farmer's cheese is dry enough to slice or crumble and is a good all-purpose cheese.

Hoop cheese is a dry drained cottage cheese, but not as dry as farmer's. It is common in Russian cooking. If it's not available in your grocery store, you might find it in a Jewish delicatessen.

Quark is a German-style soft cheese that is similar in texture and flavor to sour cream with a hint of sweetness. It comes only in lower-fat and non-fat versions, but due to natural extra flavor and texture, it's a good substitute for lower-fat sour cream and yogurt.

Provolone is a cheese of Italian origin that is aged for up to a year or more to create a mild, smoky flavor. It is good for cooking. The varieties that are aged the longest are firm enough to grate.

Ricotta is an Italian-style soft fresh cheese made with the by-products of provolone and mozzarella. It is a standard ingredient in lasagna, manicotti and cheesecake. Ricotta comes in whole milk, lower-fat and non-fat varieties. I use the whole milk variety. If there is a build up of liquid on top when you open the container, I suggest draining it over a piece of cheesecloth for one hour or overnight in the refrigerator.

Mascarpone is an Italian double or triple cream cheese. The delicate, buttery texture is delicious with fruit, but it is very versatile and found in both savory and sweet recipes.

FLAVORED CHEESE
Ripened for flavor and texture

Cheddar is a firm ripened cheese that can be mild to sharp in flavor. In color, it ranges from white to orange. (Orange cheddar get its color from annatto, a natural dye.) It is popular served plain with crackers, cooked in casseroles and sauces or shredded as a garnish.

Swiss, which is ripened to a light yellow with distinctive holes, is styled after the famous cheeses made in Switzerland, Gruyère and Emmentaler. The nutty flavor makes them popular in sandwiches and cooking.

Blue cheese is aptly named because it has blue veins running through it — a result of being treated with molds and ripened. The aging process intensifies the flavor of the cheese, which is popular in salads and salad dressings and served with fruit. It is also used in cooking. The texture is firm enough for crumbling. My favorite is Maytag Blue® from Iowa. Well-known names for international blue cheeses include Gorgonzola from Italy, Stilton from England and Roquefort from France.

Parmesan is ripened for two or more years to a hard, dry state, which makes it perfect for grating or shaving. The rich, sharp flavor of the premium aged versions imported from Italy is easily distinguished from that of the grocery store pre-grated brands.

CHOCOLATE

Whenever I'm asked what brand of chocolate I like, I always say that chocolate is like wine. Some people prefer white, some reds. Pastry chefs generally lean toward rich French chocolate while others love the creamy Belgian and even American artesian chocolates. I say go with a good-quality brand that has a high percentage of cocoa butter and no tropical oils and you can't lose.

I tend to stay clear of chip varieties in my recipes as they do not melt easily and are better used in cookies and quick desserts.

BAKING, BITTER OR UNSWEETENED CHOCOLATE

Use this type of chocolate when you're baking something with a lot of sugar. It is the only chocolate I melt in the microwave because it doesn't have any sugar to cook faster than the chocolate. You can still burn it, though, so be careful.

BITTERSWEET, SEMI-SWEET OR SWEET CHOCOLATE

These chocolates can be used interchangeably in most recipes without any change to the outcome other than the taste. Bittersweet must contain at least 35% chocolate liquor (a by-product of the manufacturing of the cocoa beans into chocolate). Semi-sweet and sweet must contain at least 15 to 35% chocolate liquor.

MILK CHOCOLATE

I only use milk chocolate when I want a sweeter taste in my pastry. It cannot be used interchangeably with other chocolates. Melt over steam from a double boiler only and not over direct heat. Milk chocolate must contain at least 12% milk solids and 10% chocolate liquor.

WHITE CHOCOLATE

Not really a chocolate, white chocolate is a mixture of cocoa butter, milk solids, vanilla and lecithin. US regulations do not allow it to be classified as chocolate because it does not contain any chocolate liquor.

COCOA POWDER

You can find this in all grocery stores. It is generally sold unsweetened.

DUTCH PROCESSED COCOA POWDER

This is a dark rich cocoa power that gives a cheesecake its glorious deep color. It is processed with alkali, which neutralizes the cocoa powder's natural acidity.

SUGAR

Sugar has many uses besides sweetening. As an ingredient in pastry dough, it adds tenderness. It adds body to help egg whites become meringues. It is a natural preservative that allows jelly and jam to have a long shelf life. Heat makes it turn brown, so it adds an attractive color to many baked goods and candy.

GRANULATED SUGAR

Granulated or white sugar is the most common form of sugar. When it is pulverized, which is easily done in a blender, it is called superfine sugar. Because superfine sugar melts so quickly, it is used for sweetening cold liquids and in delicate sweets such as meringues. When it is crushed to an even finer powder, with a bit of cornstarch added, it is called powdered sugar or confectioner's (icing) sugar, which is excellent for icings and candy or as a decoration.

BROWN SUGAR

Light and brown sugars are created when white sugar is mixed with molasses. The light variety is lighter in taste, but both have nutritional value from the molasses while white sugar has none. There's also some calcium, phosphorus, iron, potassium and sodium, making brown sugar a popular addition in cookies and cereal.

Unless a recipe specifies, you can use either light or dark. Because it is very moist and tends to clump, brown sugar should be packed tightly in a measuring cup to get the exact amount required.

Store brown sugar in an airtight container or in the refrigerator. If the sugar becomes too hard, restore its moisture by placing an apple slice in the container or by warming the sugar in a low oven with a few drops of water for 20 minutes. Granulated and liquid brown sugars are good for cereal or fruit but should not be substituted in baking recipes because of their different moisture contents.

Natural or raw sugar looks and tastes much like brown sugar, but it's not brown sugar. It is a by-product of sugarcane and is prized for having nutritional value. If it is purified, as is commonly done in the United States, the nutritional value is lost.

LIQUID SUGARS

Liquid sugars come in a variety of different flavors and can be used to add sweetness to baked goods, including cheesecake. Store in a cool, dry place for the best shelf life.

Honey is made by bees from flower nectar and therefore is a natural sugar, but that doesn't mean it has fewer calories. It actually has a few more. Because it is sweeter, use less honey if substituting it for other liquid sweeteners.

Molasses made from sugarcane or sugar beet syrup is available in three varieties: light, dark and blackstrap. Light molasses is typically used as table syrup, while dark molasses provides the distinctive sweet flavor of gingerbread and Boston baked beans. Blackstrap molasses is only slightly more nutritious than the other versions and not commonly used in baking.

Corn syrup is made from cornstarch and is available in light and dark varieties. Popular in baking, it does not crystallize and it makes baked products brown more quickly than granulated sugar. The dark version is best used when color doesn't matter and the caramel flavor is an asset to the recipe. Both types are used as table syrups and in frostings, candy and jam.

EGGS

The recipes in this book were tested using large eggs. Eggs are easier to separate when cold. After separating, allow eggs to come to room temperature before using. Leftover whites and yolks will keep for up to two days in a covered container in the refrigerator. Both can be frozen as well. Store eggs in the carton in which they came in the refrigerator for up to a month.

NUTS

Nuts provide nutritional value, including a generous amount of the good monounsaturated fat. But because of the fat content, they have the corresponding calories, too. They add flavor and texture to baked goods. Refrigerate or freeze shelled nuts that won't be used right away. For the best results, defrost and toast before proceeding with the recipe.

To toast nuts, preheat the oven to 350°F (180°C). Spread the nuts on a cookie sheet and bake for 10 to 12 minutes, checking a few times to make sure they don't burn. Allow to cool before chopping. Some nuts may require longer baking, just be careful to watch that they do not burn.

COOKIES AND CRACKERS FOR CRUSTS

Making crusts from cookies and crackers is easily done in a food processor or with a rolling pin. If using a food processor, place whole cookies in a work bowl fitted with a metal blade and pulse on and off until the crumbs feel like wet sand. There is no need to remove the center filling of a sandwich cookie. If using a rolling pin, put cookies or crackers in a plastic bag and grind using a rolling action. Many recipes call for $1\frac{1}{2}$ cups (375 mL) of crumbs to make a 9-inch (23 cm) cheesecake crust. Here are some measurements that make that amount:

- 20 graham cracker squares
- 45 vanilla wafers
- 15 chocolate sandwich cookies
- 30 Ritz®-style crackers

FLAVORINGS AND SPICES

OILS AND EXTRACTS

Pure vanilla extract is created by soaking vanilla beans in bourbon or vodka and then aging the liquid. The flavor and aroma are unmistakable. (See Sources, page 185, for sources of vanilla.)

Imitation vanilla is created with man-made products and barely resembles what it attempts to imitate. Despite being half the cost of the real thing, it is not worth substituting for pure vanilla extract.

Almond oil is made by pressing the oil from sweet almonds. The best versions are imported from France and have the aroma and flavor of toasted almonds. Almond extract is made from almond oil and alcohol and should be used carefully as the flavor is very intense.

Lemon oil and orange oil are made from the oils of the skins of the citrus fruits. Their base is oil rather than alcohol, which is found in extracts. A small amount delivers a lot of flavor.

Mint is grown in many varieties but the two most common flavors for extracts and oils used in baking are spearmint and peppermint.

SPICES

Indispensable spices for savory and sweet cheesecakes are cinnamon, cloves, poppy seeds, nutmeg, allspice and citrus zest. Spices go stale all too quickly, especially the finely ground ones. If they are no longer fragrant, discard. Keep spices tightly sealed and store in a cool, dry, dark place. For the best flavor, purchase whole spices and grind them as you need them.

HERBS

The herbs most frequently used in savory cheesecakes are basil, tarragon, thyme and rosemary. Dried herbs are more intensely flavored than fresh, so if you must substitute dried for fresh, use half as much as the recipe specifies. Dried herbs go stale quickly, especially the finely ground ones. When a herb loses its aroma, be ruthless and discard. Keep herbs in tightly closed containers and store in a cool, dry, dark place.

Basic Techniques for Perfect Cheesecake

PREPARATION IS KEY

To make a perfect cheesecake every time, prepare like a professional. Get all the ingredients out and on the counter. Unless you live in a very hot climate allow the cold ingredients, such as eggs and cheese, to sit out for about three hours or until they reach room temperature. This will ensure easy and thorough mixing with no lumps. Prepare all the other ingredients, measuring each one so that it's ready to use. Don't wait to toast and chop nuts until they are called for in the recipe. Preparing ahead saves many greasy hands on the refrigerator door fumbling for a forgotten item or discovering that you need to go to the store.

THOROUGH BLENDING TECHNIQUE

Thorough mixing is the second critical step for perfect cheesecake. Use the paddle attachment, not the whip, on a stand mixer. Beat the cream cheese thoroughly. Add the sugar slowly and beat in thoroughly, making sure that there are no lumps and that the mixture looks creamy, not granular. Watch the sides of the bowl and the paddle for cheese that has adhered and scrape down both with a rubber spatula.

Add the eggs one at a time and beat well after each addition. Stop the mixer occasionally and carefully scrape down the bowl to make sure that nothing is left on the sides or bottom.

WHIPPING TECHNIQUE

Cream

To whip cream, use chilled cream in a cold bowl and a hand-held mixer with cold beaters or a cold whisk. Whip the chilled cream on medium-high speed until it thickens, then lower the speed and continue whipping until soft peaks or firm peaks form, as specified in the recipe. Be careful after the soft-peak stage as cream turns to butter if overbeaten, and you will have to start over. Only whipping cream, or heavy cream, has a milk fat content of 35%, which is high enough to allow it to become whipped cream. Half-and-half will not whip properly.

Egg Whites

To whip egg whites to form soft peaks, begin with a spotless metal or glass bowl and whisk or hand-held mixer. Any grease in the bowl or on the whisk, and any egg yolk in the whites, will ruin your effort. Start over if you break a yolk and wash the tools beforehand to be sure they are grease-free. Eggs separate more easily when cold, but allow the whites to sit on the counter after separating and don't beat them until they have reached room temperature.

Adding Flavors

Extracts and oils can be poured directly into the batter to blend. Melted chocolate must be cooled before it is added to the main mixture. First, stir a small amount of the batter into the container with the melted chocolate. This will help the ingredients to combine into a finer batter.

OVEN TEMPERATURE AND RACK CHECK

When making cheesecake, always preheat the oven and place the rack in the center of the oven. Perfect cheesecake requires accurate oven temperatures. Check your oven temperature for accuracy against an oven thermometer. To do this, preheat the oven to 350°F (180°C) for 15 minutes. Place an independent oven thermometer inside for a few minutes, then take a reading. If it indicates that the oven is above or below 350°F (180°C), either recalibrate the oven or rely on the thermometer and adjust your control setting until 350°F (180°C) is attained. It is not difficult to recalibrate an oven. If your owner's manual does not have instructions, contact a repairperson.

IT'S DONE WHEN IT JIGGLES

Bake the cheesecake in the center of the oven for 45 to 55 minutes or until the top starts to brown lightly. When you pull out the oven rack to remove the cheesecake, the center of the cheesecake should have a slight jiggle to it, with the sides looking somewhat dry. Don't worry about the wobbling center — the cheesecake will continue to bake as it cools and the center will firm up.

GETTING IT OUT OF THE PAN
Cheesecake Pan
To unmold the cheesecake from a cheesecake pan, first run a warm wet cloth over the outside. Then run a small spatula between the cheesecake and the pan, being careful not to scrape the metal pan. Place a heavy can on the counter with the cheesecake pan on top. Press the sides of the pan downward. The cheesecake will be left sitting on the disc. Have a serving platter close by. Insert a large offset spatula between the disc and the cheesecake crust to loosen the cake. Slide the cake onto the platter.

Springform Pan
To unmold the cheesecake from a springform pan, first run a warm wet cloth over the outside. Then run a small spatula between the cheesecake and the pan, being careful not to scrape the metal pan. Carefully release the spring latch. Have a serving platter close by. Insert a large offset spatula between the metal lip and the cheesecake crust to loosen the cake. Slide the cheesecake onto the platter.

STORING AND FREEZING
Proper Storage for Maintaining Flavor
After the cheesecake has cooled on a rack for two hours, cover it tightly with plastic wrap and refrigerate for at least six hours or overnight before serving. Refrigerate leftovers after serving.

Wrapping for the Freezer and Getting It Out on Time to Serve
After covering the cheesecake tightly with plastic wrap, wrap it again in foil. Cheesecake freezes well for up to three months. To serve, take it out of the freezer and allow it to defrost in the refrigerator for 24 hours.

TROUBLESHOOTING
To prevent cracking
Allow all ingredients to come to room temperature before using. Incorporate eggs one at a time. Preheat oven to 350°F (180°C). Remove the cheesecake from the oven while the center still jiggles.

To prevent a grainy texture
Allow fat, cream cheese or butter to come to room temperature before beating. Add sugar, slowly and beating well until incorporated and dissolved. Scrape the sides of the bowl often to make sure there are no lumps.

To prevent overbaking and dryness
Remove the cheesecake from the oven while the center still jiggles. A firm center in a hot cheesecake means it is overcooked.

Solutions to underbaking
You can always put the cheesecake back in the oven for a few more minutes if the center seems more liquid than jiggling. Most underbaking errors can be remedied by refrigerating before serving.

Frequently Asked Questions from My Cheesecake Classes

WHY DO CHEESECAKES CRACK?

One great myth about cheesecakes is that cracks or crevices are often caused by drafts inside the oven or during the cooling process. The truth is simply that eggs are proteins, which create pockets in the fat that explode when exposed to heat. Slowly adding the eggs one at a time and beating well after each addition will help eliminate the pockets and the resulting crevices.

It is also important to allow all ingredients to come to room temperature, to preheat the oven to 350°F (180°C) and to remove the cheesecake from the oven while the center still jiggles. If the center does split or crack, use a decorative topping to cover. The cheesecake will still taste wonderful.

DO I HAVE TO BAKE THE CRUST FIRST?

Most recipes do not require baking first. The best place for the crust is in the freezer until the filling is ready to be poured into it. If the crust is properly made in a cheesecake pan, it will not stick. It is not necessary to grease the pan unless you're using a springform pan (see page 10).

HOW DO YOU GET THE WHITE ICING OUT OF THE CHOCOLATE SANDWICH COOKIES TO MAKE THE CRUST?

It would be fun to eat it out, but unnecessary. Put whole chocolate sandwich cookies, icing and all, in a food processor and pulse on and off until crumbs form. The icing disappears like magic.

CAN I FREEZE A CHEESECAKE?

Wrapped properly to be airtight, in plastic wrap and an outer covering of foil, cheesecake suffers no loss of texture for up to three months in the freezer. Allow it to defrost in the refrigerator for 24 hours before serving. Decorate and refrigerate two hours before serving.

CAN I MAKE DIET CHEESECAKE?

Absolutely, by following the reduced-calorie recipes in this book. Substituting non-fat products to create your own recipes is not recommended as other adjustments must be made to compensate for moisture content and lack of fat.

HOW CAN I MAKE PERFECT-LOOKING CHEESECAKES?

Most perfect-looking cheesecakes are decorated with whipped cream and other items. It's called "finishing off" the cake. Throughout this book, I provide instructions on how to finish off a cake to make it look perfect!

Flavored and Vanilla Cheesecakes

Blue Ribbon

CHEESECAKE

> I have won numerous awards with this recipe, also affectionately called "Patty's Favorite Cheesecake" after my mom, my biggest fan.

SERVES 10 TO 12

TIPS
Zest lemons and limes before juicing and freeze the zest for another recipe.

This cheesecake freezes well for up to 4 months before decorating. Defrost in the refrigerator the day prior to use and then decorate.

VARIATION
If fresh berries are not available, spread 1 cup (250 mL) strawberry preserves on top.

Preheat oven to 350°F (180°C)
9-inch (23 cm) cheesecake pan, ungreased, or springform pan with 3-inch (7.5 cm) sides, greased (for other pan sizes, see page 10)

CRUST

1¼ cups	graham cracker crumbs	300 mL
¼ cup	unsalted butter, melted	50 mL

FILLING

4	packages (each 8 oz/250 g) cream cheese, softened	4
1¼ cups	granulated sugar	300 mL
4	eggs	4
3 tbsp	fresh lemon juice	45 mL
1 tsp	vanilla	5 mL

TOPPING

½ cup	sour cream	125 mL
¼ cup	granulated sugar	50 mL
1 tbsp	fresh lemon juice	15 mL
½ tsp	vanilla	2 mL

DECORATION

2 cups	fresh strawberries, sliced	500 mL

1. CRUST: In a medium bowl, combine graham cracker crumbs and butter. Press into bottom of cheesecake pan and freeze.

2. FILLING: In a large mixer bowl, beat cream cheese and sugar on medium-high speed for 3 minutes. Add eggs, one at a time, beating after each addition. Stir in lemon juice and vanilla. Pour over frozen crust. Bake in preheated oven for 45 to 55 or until the top is light brown and the center has a slight jiggle to it. Cool on the counter for 10 minutes (do not turn the oven off). The cake will sink slightly.

3. TOPPING: In a small bowl, combine sour cream, sugar, lemon juice and vanilla. Pour into center of cooled cake and spread out to edges. Bake for 5 minutes more. Cool on a rack for 2 hours. Cover with plastic wrap and refrigerate for at least 6 hours before decorating.

4. DECORATION: Top with sliced strawberries when completely chilled.

New York Style

CHEESECAKE

In my first pastry job, I made a New York style cheesecake. I never knew what it meant until I stepped into a deli in Manhattan, a Mecca for cheesecake fans.

SERVES 10 TO 12

TIP
Save leftover egg whites or egg yolks by freezing them for up to 6 months. Freeze them in an ice-cube tray. When frozen, pop them out and place cubes in plastic freezer bags.

VARIATION
You can replace the lemon and orange zest with 1 tsp (5 mL) rum extract for a different taste.

Preheat oven to 500°F (260°C)
9-inch (23 cm) cheesecake pan, ungreased, or springform pan with 3-inch (7.5 cm) sides, greased (for other pan sizes, see page 10)

CRUST

1½ cups	graham cracker crumbs	375 mL
¼ cup	unsalted butter, melted	50 mL

FILLING

5	packages (each 8 oz/250 g) cream cheese, softened	5
1¼ cups	granulated sugar	300 mL
3 tbsp	all-purpose flour	45 mL
1½ tsp	lemon zest	7 mL
1½ tsp	orange zest	7 mL
5	eggs	5
2	egg yolks	2
1 tsp	vanilla	5 mL
¼ cup	whipping (35%) cream	50 mL

1. CRUST: In a large bowl, combine graham cracker crumbs and butter. Press into bottom of cheesecake pan and freeze.

2. FILLING: In a large mixer bowl, beat cream cheese and sugar on medium speed for 3 minutes. Mix in flour, lemon and orange zest. Add eggs and egg yolks, one at a time, beating after each addition. Mix in vanilla and cream. Pour batter over frozen crust. Bake for only 10 minutes at 500°F (260°C), reduce heat to 200°F (100°C). Bake for an additional 60 minutes. The top should be puffy like a soufflé with a light golden color. Cool on a rack for 2 hours. Cover with plastic wrap and refrigerate for at least 6 hours before serving.

Citrus Daiquiri

CHEESECAKE

SERVES 10 TO 12

TIPS
Zest lemons and limes before juicing.

To save time purchase shelled pistachios. Shelled pistachios can be stored in the refrigerator up to 3 months, but are not a good candidate for freezing. The more economical unshelled nuts can be stored for 3 months in the refrigerator or up to 1 year in the freezer. Buy green pistachios and not the dyed red ones.

VARIATION
You can use ¼ tsp (1 mL) rum extract instead of the rum liqueur. A non-alcoholic substitute for rum is orange juice concentrate.

Preheat oven to 350°F (180°C)
9-inch (23 cm) cheesecake pan, ungreased, or springform pan with 3-inch (7.5 cm) sides, greased (for other pan sizes, see page 10)

CRUST

1 cup	graham cracker crumbs	250 mL
¼ cup	chopped pistachio nuts	50 mL
¼ cup	unsalted butter, melted	50 mL

FILLING

4	packages (each 8 oz/250 g) cream cheese, softened	4
1 cup	granulated sugar	250 mL
4	eggs	4
¼ cup	rum	50 mL
2 tsp	each lime and lemon zest	10 mL
3 tbsp	fresh lime juice	45 mL
2 tbsp	fresh lemon juice	25 mL
1 tbsp	cornstarch	15 mL

TOPPING

½ cup	sour cream	125 mL
1½ tbsp	granulated sugar	22 mL
½ tsp	each lemon and lime zest	2 mL

DECORATION

⅓ cup	chopped pistachio nuts	75 mL

1. CRUST: In a bowl, combine graham cracker crumbs, nuts and butter. Press into bottom of cheesecake pan and freeze.

2. FILLING: In a large mixer bowl, beat cream cheese and sugar on medium-high speed for 3 minutes. Add eggs, one at a time, beating after each addition. Stir in rum, lime and lemon zest, lime and lemon juice and cornstarch. Pour over frozen crust. Bake in preheated oven for 45 to 55 minutes or until the top is light brown and the center has a slight jiggle to it. Cool on the counter for 10 minutes (do not turn the oven off). The cake will sink slightly.

3. TOPPING: In a bowl, combine sour cream, sugar and zests. Pour into center of cooled cake and spread to edges. Bake 5 minutes more. Cool on a rack for 2 hours. Cover with plastic wrap and refrigerate for 6 hours before decorating.

4. DECORATION: Sprinkle pistachios in a 1-inch (2.5 cm) border around top of cake.

Double Orange

CHEESECAKE ✒

A French orange
liqueur hints at the
taste and aroma of
oranges in every bite.
✒

SERVES 10 TO 12

TIP
To drain ricotta,
place a fine mesh
strainer over a bowl,
place the cheese in
the strainer and let
stand for at least
1 hour or overnight
in the refrigerator.

VARIATION
Use frozen orange
juice concentrate
instead of the liqueur.

Preheat oven to 350°F (180°C)
9-inch (23 cm) cheesecake pan, ungreased, or springform pan
with 3-inch (7.5 cm) sides, greased (for other pan sizes, see page 10)

CRUST

1 ½ cups	graham cracker crumbs	375 mL
¼ cup	unsalted butter, melted	50 mL

FILLING

1 lb	ricotta cheese, drained (see Tip, left)	500 g
1	package (8 oz/250 g) cream cheese, softened	1
1 cup	granulated sugar	250 mL
4	egg yolks	4
¼ cup	all-purpose flour	50 mL
½ tsp	salt	2 mL
½ cup	whipping (35%) cream	125 mL
1 tsp	orange zest	5 mL
4 oz	orange liqueur	125 mL
4	egg whites	4

DECORATION

Classic Whipped Cream Topping
(see recipe, page 172)

1. CRUST: In a medium bowl, mix graham cracker crumbs and butter. Press into bottom of cheesecake pan and freeze.

2. FILLING: In a large mixer bowl, beat ricotta, cream cheese and sugar on medium-high speed for 3 minutes. Add egg yolks, one at a time, beating after each addition. Mix in flour, salt, cream, orange zest and orange liqueur. In a clean bowl, whip egg whites until firm. With a rubber spatula, fold egg whites into batter. Pour over frozen crust. Bake in preheated oven for 45 to 55 minutes or until the top is light brown and the center has a slight jiggle to it. Cool on a rack for 2 hours. Cover with plastic wrap and refrigerate for at least 6 hours before decorating or serving.

3. DECORATION: Ice top of cake with Classic Whipped Cream Topping or pipe a ribbon around border, if desired.

Chocolate Cookie

CHEESECAKE

SERVES 10 TO 12

TIPS
This recipe takes less than one pound (500 g) of the cookies. You can eat the rest! Cookies with double filling made into crumbs have enough moisture in them to omit the butter in the crust.

If the wall of cookies start to fall, do not worry, you can prop them up when you pour the filling in pan.

VARIATION
During Halloween you can find chocolate sandwich cookies with orange centers. These would make a great spooky dessert.

Preheat oven to 350°F (180°C)
9-inch (23 cm) cheesecake pan, ungreased, or springform pan with 3-inch (7.5 cm) sides, greased (for other pan sizes, see page 10)

CRUST

1¼ cups	chocolate sandwich cookie crumbs	300 mL
¼ cup	unsalted butter, melted	50 mL
10	chocolate sandwich cookies	10

FILLING

3	packages (each 8 oz/250 g) cream cheese, softened	3
1 cup	sour cream	250 mL
¾ cup	granulated sugar	175 mL
4	eggs	4
2 tsp	vanilla	10 mL
4	chocolate sandwich cookies, quartered	4

DECORATION

Classic Whipped Cream Topping
(see recipe, page 172)

1. CRUST: In a medium bowl, combine cookie crumbs and butter. Press into cheesecake pan. Cut sandwich cookies in half at the cream filling. Place each half, cookie side, against side of pan, one after another creating a wall of chocolate sandwich cookies. Set aside in the freezer to firm.

2. FILLING: In a large mixer bowl, beat cream cheese, sour cream and sugar on medium-high speed for 3 minutes. Add eggs, one at a time, beating after each addition. Stir in vanilla. Fold in quartered cookies. Pour batter over frozen crust. Bake in preheated oven for 45 to 55 minutes or until the top is light brown and the center has a slight jiggle to it. Cool on a rack for 2 hours. Cover with plastic wrap and refrigerate for at least 6 hours before decorating.

3. DECORATION: Ice top of cake with Classic Whipped Cream Topping. Top with chocolate sandwich cookies.

Minty Chocolate

CHEESECAKE

SERVES 10 TO 12

TIPS
Purchase chocolate
in bar form rather
than chips for the
melted semi-sweet
chocolate in this
recipe.

When making cookie
crumbs, you do not
have to scrape the
cream filling out of
the cookie, just place
all into the food
processor and pulse.

VARIATION
Substitute mint chips
for semi-sweet
chips and delete the
peppermint extract.

Preheat oven to 350°F (180°C)
9-inch (23 cm) cheesecake pan, ungreased, or springform pan
with 3-inch (7.5 cm) sides, greased (for other pan sizes, see page 10)

CRUST

1½ cups	chocolate sandwich cookie crumbs	375 mL
¼ cup	unsalted butter, melted	50 mL

FILLING

3	packages (each 8 oz/250 g) cream cheese, softened	3
¾ cup	granulated sugar	175 mL
3	eggs	3
¼ cup	all-purpose flour	50 mL
½ cup	sour cream	125 mL
1 tsp	vanilla	5 mL
¼ tsp	peppermint extract	1 mL
3 oz	semi-sweet chocolate, melted and cooled	90 g
1 cup	semi-sweet chocolate chips	250 mL
2 tsp	all-purpose flour	10 mL

1. CRUST: In a medium bowl, combine cookie crumbs and butter. Press into bottom of cheesecake pan and freeze.

2. FILLING: In a large mixer bowl, beat cream cheese and sugar on medium-high speed for 3 minutes. Add eggs, one at a time, beating after each addition. Mix in ¼ cup (50 mL) flour. Mix in sour cream, vanilla and peppermint. While the mixer is running, pour in melted and cooled chocolate in a steady stream. In a small bowl, combine chocolate chips and remaining flour. Toss into batter. Pour batter over frozen crust. Bake in preheated oven for 45 to 55 minutes or until the top is light brown and the center has a slight jiggle to it. Cool on a rack for 2 hours. Cover with plastic wrap and refrigerate for at least 6 hours before serving.

Café au Lait

CHEESECAKE

The richness of coffee, chocolate and hazelnuts make this cheesecake a winner for the fall season.

SERVES 10 TO 12

TIPS
Toasting brings out the natural oils and flavor of nuts. Place nuts in a single layer on a baking sheet. Bake at 350°F (180°C) for 10 to 12 minutes or until fragrant.

Neufchâtel cheese is a reduced-fat cream cheese that contains 23% milk fat, which means a few less calories. You could also use a light cream cheese.

Preheat oven to 350°F (180°C)
9-inch (23 cm) cheesecake pan, ungreased, or springform pan
with 3-inch (7.5 cm) sides, greased (for other pan sizes, see page 10)

CRUST

1 1/2 cups	chocolate sandwich cookie crumbs	375 mL
1/4 cup	packed light brown sugar	50 mL
1 tsp	instant espresso powder	5 mL
1/2 tsp	ground cinnamon	2 mL
1/3 cup	unsalted butter, melted	75 mL

FILLING

2 tbsp	milk	25 mL
1 1/2 tsp	instant espresso powder	7 mL
2 tbsp	unsalted butter	25 mL
2	packages (each 8 oz/250 g) Neufchâtel cheese (see Tip, left)	2
1	package (8 oz/250 g) cream cheese, softened	1
2/3 cup	granulated sugar	150 mL
4	eggs	4
1/4 cup	milk	50 mL
1/3 cup	hazelnuts, chopped and toasted	75 mL
2 tbsp	coffee-flavored liqueur	25 mL

DECORATION

1	Coffee-Flavored Syrup (see recipe, page 179)	1
1/3 cup	hazelnuts, chopped and toasted	75 mL

1. **CRUST:** In a food processor, pulse crumbs, sugar, espresso powder and cinnamon until fine. Pour butter through feed tube and pulse until combined. Press into pan and freeze.

2. **FILLING:** In a saucepan, heat 2 tbsp (25 mL) milk, espresso powder and butter until butter melts. Set aside. In a large bowl, beat Neufchâtel cheese, cream cheese and sugar on medium-high for 3 minutes. Add eggs, one at a time, beating after each addition. Reduce to low, add milk, hazelnuts, liqueur and espresso mixture. Pour over frozen crust. Bake for 45 to 55 minutes or until the top is light brown. Cool for 2 hours. Cover and refrigerate for 6 hours before decorating.

3. **DECORATION:** Place a slice on a plate. Pour 2 tbsp (25 mL) Coffee-Flavored Syrup on top and sprinkle with hazelnuts.

Coffee Liqueur

CHEESECAKE

SERVES 10 TO 12

TIP
You may have to add additional butter to the crust depending on the brand of cookies. Just make sure the crust is like wet sand.

VARIATION
Using mascarpone cheese instead of sour cream will yield an even richer, creamier cake.

Preheat oven to 325°F (160°C)
9-inch (23 cm) cheesecake pan, ungreased, or springform pan with 3-inch (7.5 cm) sides, greased (for other pan sizes, see page 10)

CRUST

1 1/3 cups	chocolate sandwich cookie crumbs	325 mL
1/4 cup	unsalted butter, melted	50 mL

FILLING

2	packages (each 8 oz/250 g) cream cheese, softened	2
1/3 cup	granulated sugar	75 mL
1/4 tsp	salt	1 mL
1 cup	sour cream	250 mL
3	eggs	3
1/4 cup	coffee-flavored liqueur	50 mL
2 tbsp	unsalted butter, melted	25 mL

DECORATION

Coffee-Flavored Syrup
(see recipe, page 179)

1. CRUST: In a medium bowl, mix cookie crumbs and butter. Press into bottom of cheesecake pan and freeze.

2. FILLING: In a large mixer bowl, beat cream cheese and sugar on medium high for 3 minutes. Blend in salt and sour cream. Add eggs, one at a time, beating after each addition. Blend in liqueur and melted butter. Pour batter over frozen crust. Bake in preheated oven for 40 to 50 minutes or until the top is light brown and the center has a slight jiggle to it. Cool on a rack for 2 hours. Cover with plastic wrap and refrigerate for at least 6 hours before decorating or serving.

3. DECORATION: When ready to serve, pour about 2 tbsp (25 mL) Coffee-Flavored Syrup on individual plates and position piece of cake on top.

Espresso

CHEESECAKE

SERVES 10 TO 12

TIP
Shaved chocolate looks great on this cheesecake. You can create chocolate shavings by moving a spatula in an up and down motion on the side of a large chocolate bar or with a potato peeler on a cold chocolate bar.

Preheat oven to 325°F (160°C)
9-inch (23 cm) cheesecake pan, ungreased, or springform pan with 3-inch (7.5 cm) sides, greased (for other pan sizes, see page 10)

CRUST

1½ cups	hazelnuts, toasted and chopped	375 mL
⅓ cup	granulated sugar	75 mL
1 tbsp	unsweetened cocoa powder	15 mL
3 tbsp	unsalted butter, melted	45 mL

FILLING

1 cup	brewed espresso	250 mL
3	packages (each 8 oz/250 g) cream cheese, softened	3
1⅓ cups	granulated sugar	325 mL
3	eggs	3
3	egg yolks	3
1½ tbsp	cornstarch	22 mL
¼ tsp	salt	1 mL
⅓ cup	whipping (35%) cream	75 mL
2 tsp	lemon zest	10 mL
1 tbsp	fresh lemon juice	15 mL
1 tbsp	coffee-flavored liqueur	15 mL
1 tsp	vanilla	5 mL

DECORATION

½ cup	whipping (35%) cream	125 mL
2 tbsp	granulated sugar	25 mL
12	candied coffee beans	12

VARIATION
Substitute pecans if
hazelnuts are difficult
to find.

1. CRUST: In a food processor, fitted with a metal blade, pulse hazelnuts, sugar and cocoa powder until fine. Pour melted butter through the feed tube and pulse until combined. Press into bottom of cheesecake pan. Place in 325°F (160°C) oven for 10 minutes. Set aside. Increase oven temperature to 350°F (180°C).

2. FILLING: In a small saucepan, boil espresso until it reduces to 1/4 cup (50 mL). Cool completely. In a large mixer bowl, beat cream cheese and sugar on medium-high speed for 3 minutes. Mix in whole eggs and egg yolks, one at a time, beating after each addition. Mix in cornstarch and salt. Reduce to low speed and add reduced espresso, cream, lemon zest, lemon juice, coffee-flavored liqueur and vanilla. Pour batter over crust. Bake in preheated oven for 60 to 75 minutes or until the top is light brown and the center has a slight jiggle to it. Cool on a rack for 2 hours. Cover with plastic wrap and refrigerate for at least 6 hours before decorating or serving.

3. DECORATION: In a well-chilled bowl, whip cream on medium-high speed until soft peaks form. With the mixer still running, sprinkle sugar into cream and continue whipping until firm peaks form. Ice top of cake with whipped cream or pipe rosettes around top of cake, if desired. Top with candied coffee beans.

Creamy Amaretto

CHEESECAKE

When touring the Banff Springs area in the 1980s I came across a light almond cheesecake. This is just like the one served to me on that cold fall evening.

SERVES 10 TO 12

TIPS
Process graham crackers and almonds together in a food processor fitted with a metal blade to avoid making almond butter. A few tablespoons (25 mL) flour mixed in with nuts works well too if there are no crumbs in the recipe.

For a smoother texture, purée the cottage cheese in a food processor before adding to filling.

VARIATION
Substitute 1 tsp (5 mL) almond extract for the liqueur.

Preheat oven to 350°F (180°C)
9-inch (23 cm) cheesecake pan, ungreased, or springform pan with 3-inch (7.5 cm) sides, greased (for other pan sizes, see page 10)

CRUST

1 1/4 cups	graham cracker crumbs	300 mL
1/4 cup	almonds, toasted and coarsely ground	50 mL
1/4 cup	unsalted butter, melted	50 mL

FILLING

3	packages (each 8 oz/250 g) cream cheese, softened	3
8 oz	small curd cottage cheese (see Tip, left)	250 g
1 1/2 cups	granulated sugar	375 mL
1/2 tsp	salt	2 mL
4	eggs	4
1 tsp	orange zest	5 mL
4 oz	almond liqueur	125 mL

DECORATION

	Classic Whipped Cream Topping (see recipe, page 172)	
1/3 cup	almond slivers, toasted	75 mL

1. CRUST: In a medium bowl, mix graham cracker crumbs, almonds and butter. Press into bottom of cheesecake pan and freeze.

2. FILLING: In a large mixer bowl, beat cream cheese and cottage cheese on medium-high speed for 3 minutes. Mix in sugar and salt. Add eggs, one at a time, beating after each addition. Blend in orange zest and almond liqueur. Pour batter over crust. Bake in preheated oven for 45 to 55 minutes or until the top is light brown and the center has a slight jiggle to it. Cool on a rack for 2 hours. Cover with plastic wrap and refrigerate for at least 6 hours before decorating or serving.

3. DECORATION: Ice top of cake with Classic Whipped Cream Topping or pipe rosettes around top of cake, if desired. Sprinkle with toasted almonds.

Farmer's

CHEESECAKE

SERVES 10 TO 12

TIP
To preserve a big harvest of lemons, I zest all of my lemons on one day to break down the walls of the lemon; the next day I juice them. Store the zest in plastic bags in the freezer. Freeze the juice in ice-cube trays. When frozen, pop them out and store the cubes in plastic freezer bags.

VARIATION
If your supermarket doesn't stock farmer's cheese, try a specialty store or substitute small curd cottage cheese, drained.

Preheat the oven to 325°F (160°C)
9-inch (23 cm) cheesecake pan, ungreased, or springform pan with 3-inch (7.5 cm) sides, greased (for other pan sizes, see page 10)

CRUST

2 cups	butter cookie crumbs	500 mL
1 cup	granulated sugar	250 mL
1/4 cup	walnuts, chopped	50 mL
1 tsp	ground cinnamon	5 mL
1/2 cup	unsalted butter, melted	125 mL

FILLING

1/2 cup	unsalted butter, softened	125 mL
4	egg yolks	4
1 cup	granulated sugar	250 mL
2 lbs	farmer's cheese	1 kg
1 tbsp	lemon zest	15 mL
1/4 cup	fresh lemon juice	50 mL
1/4 cup	all-purpose flour	50 mL
1 tsp	vanilla	5 mL
1 tsp	baking powder	5 mL
4	egg whites	4
2 tbsp	granulated sugar	25 mL

DECORATION

1/4 cup	walnuts, chopped	50 mL

1. CRUST: In a medium bowl, combine cookie crumbs and sugar. Add walnuts and cinnamon. Add butter and stir. Press about half of crust mixture into bottom of cheesecake pan and freeze.

2. FILLING: In a large mixer bowl, beat butter, egg yolks and sugar on medium speed for 3 minutes. Add cheese, zest, lemon juice, flour, vanilla and baking powder. Set aside. In clean bowl, whip egg whites to frothy, sprinkle in sugar as you continue to whip the egg whites to the firm stage. Fold egg whites into cheese mixture. Pour batter over frozen crust. Crumble remainder of the crust mixture over filling. Bake in preheated oven for 60 to 75 minutes or until the top is light brown and the center has a slight jiggle to it. Cool on a rack for 2 hours. Cover with plastic wrap and refrigerate for at least 6 hours before decorating or serving.

3. DECORATION: Sprinkle with chopped walnuts.

Ginger and Honey

CHEESECAKE

A perfect cheesecake to finish off the flavors of an Asian-style meal. The candied and dry ginger in this cheesecake will give your taste buds a tingle.

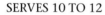

SERVES 10 TO 12

TIP
Use fresh candied ginger. It should feel soft. If the ginger is hard, soften it in hot water for about 15 minutes prior to mincing it.

Preheat oven to 350°F (180°C)
9-inch (23 cm) cheesecake pan, ungreased, or springform pan
with 3-inch (7.5 cm) sides, greased (for other pan sizes, see page 10)

CRUST

1½ cups	gingersnap cookie crumbs	375 mL
¼ cup	unsalted butter, melted	50 mL

FILLING

2	packages (each 8 oz/250 g) cream cheese, softened	2
1 cup	sour cream	250 mL
⅓ cup	all-purpose flour	75 mL
⅔ cup	packed light brown sugar	150 mL
¼ cup	liquid honey	50 mL
2	eggs	2
2 tbsp	minced candied ginger	25 mL
½ tsp	ground ginger	2 mL
¼ tsp	ground cinnamon	1 mL

DECORATION

	Classic Whipped Cream Topping (see recipe, page 172)	
¼ tsp	ground ginger	1 mL
⅛ tsp	ground cinnamon	0.5 mL

1. CRUST: In a medium bowl, mix cookie crumbs and butter. Press into bottom of cheesecake pan and freeze.

2. FILLING: In large mixer bowl, beat cream cheese and sour cream on medium-high speed for 3 minutes. Mix in flour, brown sugar and honey until well blended, about 2 minutes. Add eggs, one at a time, beating after each addition. Add candied ginger, ground ginger and cinnamon. Pour batter over crust. Bake in preheated oven for 55 to 65 minutes or until the top is light brown and the center has a slight jiggle to it. Cool on a rack for 2 hours. Cover with plastic wrap and refrigerate for at least 6 hours before decorating or serving.

3. DECORATION: Ice top of cake with Classic Whipped Cream Topping or pipe a ribbon around border, if desired. Sprinkle with ground ginger and cinnamon.

Italian Ricotta

CHEESECAKE

U*sing a chopped pecan crust makes this cheesecake pure Italian!*

SERVES 10 TO 12

TIPS
Fresh ricotta cheese creates a huge difference in taste and texture. Find an Italian deli that makes its own ricotta.

A sugar dredger or shaker is a container with a mesh lid used for lightly dusting icing sugar, flour or cocoa for decoration.

VARIATION
Substitute 1 tsp (15 mL) almond liqueur for the almond extract or substitute 1 tsp (5 mL) vanilla.

Preheat the oven to 325°F (160°C)
9-inch (23 cm) cheesecake pan, ungreased, or springform pan
with 3-inch (7.5 cm) sides, greased (for other pan sizes, see page 10)

CRUST

1½ cups	pecans, toasted and coarsely ground	375 mL

FILLING

1½ lbs	ricotta cheese, drained (see Tip, page 25)	750 g
1 cup	granulated sugar	250 mL
¼ cup	all-purpose flour	50 mL
4	eggs	4
1 tsp	almond extract	5 mL

DECORATION

¼ cup	confectioner's (icing) sugar	50 mL

1. CRUST: Sprinkle bottom of cheesecake pan evenly with ground pecans. Set aside.

2. FILLING: In a large mixer bowl, beat ricotta cheese and sugar on medium-high speed for 3 minutes. Add flour and mix for about 3 minutes. Add eggs, one at a time, beating after each addition. Add almond extract. Pour batter over crust. Bake for 55 to 65 minutes or until the top is light brown and the center has a slight jiggle to it. Cool on a rack for 2 hours. Cover with plastic wrap and refrigerate for at least 6 hours before decorating.

3. DECORATION: After cake has chilled, dust top with a sprinkling of confectioner's sugar using a sugar dredger or flour sifter.

Mocha

CHEESECAKE

Preheat oven to 375°F (190°C)
9-inch (23 cm) cheesecake pan, ungreased, or springform pan
with 3-inch (7.5 cm) sides, greased (for other pan sizes, see page 10)

Double the
pleasure of a coffee
break with a slice of
mocha cheesecake.

SERVES 10 TO 12

TIP
If the cottage cheese
has a wet look to it,
drain the cheese
through a fine mesh
strainer. Too much
moisture will change
the texture of the
cheesecake.

CRUST

1 1/2 cups	chocolate sandwich cookie crumbs	375 mL
1/4 cup	unsalted butter, melted	50 mL

FILLING

3	packages (each 8 oz/250 g) cream cheese, softened	3
8 oz	small curd cottage cheese (see Tip, left)	250 g
1 1/2 cups	granulated sugar	375 mL
4	eggs	4
2 tbsp	instant coffee powder	25 mL
1 tbsp	hot water	15 mL
1 tsp	vanilla	5 mL

TOPPING

1 tsp	instant coffee powder	5 mL
1/2 tsp	hot water	2 mL
1/2 cup	sour cream	125 mL
1/4 cup	granulated sugar	50 mL
1 tbsp	fresh lemon juice	15 mL
1/2 tsp	vanilla	2 mL

DECORATION

1/2 cup	whipping (35%) cream	125 mL
2 tbsp	granulated sugar	25 mL
12	mocha candy coffee beans	12

VARIATION
Add 2 tbsp (25 mL) rum when adding vanilla for a little kick in flavor.

1. CRUST: In a medium bowl, combine cookie crumbs and butter. Press into bottom of cheesecake pan and freeze.

2. FILLING: In a large mixer bowl, beat cream cheese, cottage cheese and sugar on medium-high speed for 3 minutes. Add eggs, one at a time, beating after each addition. In a small bowl, dissolve coffee powder in hot water. With the mixer still running, pour coffee in a steady stream into the batter. Stir in vanilla. Pour batter over frozen crust. Bake in preheated oven for 45 to 55 minutes or until the top is light brown and the center has a slight jiggle to it. Cool on counter for 10 minutes (do not turn the oven off). The cake will sink slightly.

3. TOPPING: In a small bowl, dissolve coffee powder in water. Stir in sour cream, sugar, lemon juice and vanilla. Pour into center of cooled cake and spread out to edges. Bake for 5 minutes more. Cool on a rack for 2 hours. Cover with plastic wrap and refrigerate for at least 6 hours before decorating.

4. DECORATION: In a well-chilled bowl, whip cream on medium-high speed until soft peaks form. With the mixer still running, sprinkle sugar into cream and continue whipping until firm peaks form. Ice top of cake with whipped cream or pipe rosettes around top of cake, if desired. Top with chocolate mocha beans.

Vanilla Sour Cream

CHEESECAKE

Preheat oven to 325°F (160°C)
9-inch (23 cm) cheesecake pan, ungreased, or springform pan
with 3-inch (7.5 cm) sides, greased (for other pan sizes, see page 10)

This recipe calls for vanilla bean paste. When purchasing, you should see specks of the vanilla bean, which says authentic vanilla was used.

SERVES 10 TO 12

TIP
If you cannot locate vanilla bean paste, use a fresh vanilla bean. Split it length-wise and scrape the seeds
out first. One bean is equivalent to 1 tbsp (15 mL) paste.

CRUST

1 ½ cups	vanilla cookie crumbs	375 mL
¼ cup	unsalted butter, melted	50 mL

FILLING

3	packages (each 8 oz/250 g) cream cheese, softened	3
8 oz	small curd cottage cheese (see Tip, page 32)	250 g
1 cup	sour cream	250 mL
1 ½ cups	granulated sugar	375 mL
5	eggs	5
1 tbsp	pure vanilla bean paste (see Tip, left)	15 mL
1 tsp	lemon zest	5 mL

DECORATION

½ cup	whipping (35%) cream	125 mL
2 tbsp	granulated sugar	25 mL
1 tsp	pure vanilla bean paste	5 mL

1. CRUST: In a medium bowl, combine cookie crumbs and butter. Press into bottom of cheesecake pan and freeze.

2. FILLING: In a large mixer bowl, beat cream cheese, cottage cheese, sour cream and sugar on medium-high speed for 3 minutes. Add eggs, one at a time, beating after each addition. Mix in vanilla paste and lemon zest. Pour batter over frozen crust. Bake in preheated oven for 45 to 55 minutes or until the top is light brown and the center has a slight jiggle to it. Cool on a rack for 2 hours. Cover with plastic wrap and refrigerate for at least 6 hours before decorating or serving.

3. DECORATION: In a well-chilled bowl, whip cream on medium-high speed until soft peaks form. With the mixer still running, sprinkle sugar and bean paste into cream and continue whipping until firm peaks form. Ice top of cake with the whipped cream.

Three-Cinnamon

CHEESECAKE

Yes, three types of cinnamon in one amazing cheesecake. The real deal from Ceylon is much lighter in color and more delicate in flavor than the pungent spice sold here.

SERVES 10 TO 12

TIP
For the decorating, blend sugar and the cinnamon together prior to whipping into the cream. This will make the job easier
and it will blend faster.

VARIATION
Treat yourself to a sensory experience by trying imported brands of cinnamon. I use Penzey's Spices from Wisconsin. Check my listing of suppliers on page 185 to contact them directly.

Preheat oven to 325°F (160°C)
9-inch (23 cm) cheesecake pan, ungreased, or springform pan with 3-inch (7.5 cm) sides, greased (for other pan sizes, see page 10)

CRUST

1½ cups	butter cookie crumbs	375 mL
¼ cup	unsalted butter, melted	50 mL
1 tsp	Ceylon ground cinnamon	5 mL

FILLING

3	packages (each 8 oz/250 g) cream cheese, softened	3
8 oz	small curd cottage cheese (see Tip, page 32)	250 g
1 cup	sour cream	250 mL
1½ cups	granulated sugar	375 mL
4	eggs	4
1	egg yolk	1
1 tsp	Vietnamese ground cinnamon	5 mL
½ tsp	Ceylon ground cinnamon	2 mL
½ tsp	Korintje Cassia ground cinnamon	2 mL

DECORATION

1 cup	whipping (35%) cream	250 mL
2 tbsp	granulated sugar	25 mL
¼ tsp	Vietnamese ground cinnamon	1 mL

1. **CRUST:** In a medium bowl, combine butter cookies, butter and Ceylon cinnamon. Press into bottom of cheesecake pan and freeze.

2. **FILLING:** In a large mixer bowl, beat cream cheese, cottage cheese, sour cream and sugar on medium-high speed for 3 minutes. Add eggs and egg yolk, one at a time, beating after each addition. Blend in the three cinnamons. Pour over frozen crust. Bake for 45 to 55 minutes or until the top is light brown and the center has a slight jiggle to it. Cool on a rack for 2 hours. Cover with plastic wrap and refrigerate for at least 6 hours before decorating or serving.

3. **DECORATION:** In a well-chilled bowl, whip cream on medium-high speed until soft peaks form. With the mixer still running, sprinkle sugar and cinnamon into cream and continue whipping until firm peaks firm. Ice top of cake with whipped cream or pipe rosettes around top of cake, if desired.

Toffee Cheesecake

WITH CARAMEL SAUCE

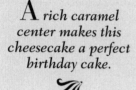

A rich caramel center makes this cheesecake a perfect birthday cake.

SERVES 10 TO 12

TIP
Keep caramel sauce at room temperature. A heavy-bottomed saucepan will avoid "hot" spots and burning caramel.

Preheat the oven to 350°F (180°C)
9-inch (23 cm) cheesecake pan, ungreased, or springform pan with 3-inch (7.5 cm) sides, greased (for other pan sizes, see page 10)

CRUST

1 ½ cups	graham cracker crumbs	375 mL
¼ cup	packed light brown sugar	50 mL
¼ cup	unsalted butter, melted	50 mL

FILLING

4	packages (each 8 oz/250 g) cream cheese, softened	4
1 cup	sour cream	250 mL
1 ¼ cups	granulated sugar	300 mL
5	eggs	5
1 tbsp	vanilla	15 mL
2 tsp	fresh lemon juice	10 mL
5 oz	toffee candy bar, crushed	150 g

TOPPING

1 ¼ cups	granulated sugar	300 mL
⅓ cup	water	75 mL
1 cup	whipping (35%) cream, room temperature	250 mL
½ cup	unsalted butter, softened	125 mL
1 tsp	vanilla	5 mL

DECORATION

¾ cup	whipping (35%) cream	175 mL
2 tbsp	granulated sugar	25 mL

VARIATION
You can omit the caramel sauce topping and call it a Toffee Candy Cheesecake.

1. CRUST: In a medium bowl, combine graham cracker crumbs, brown sugar and butter. Press into bottom of cheesecake pan and freeze.

2. FILLING: In a large mixer bowl, beat cream cheese, sour cream and sugar on medium-high speed for 3 minutes. Add eggs, one at a time, beating after each addition. Mix in vanilla and lemon juice. Fold in crushed candy bar pieces. Pour batter over frozen crust. Bake in preheated oven for 45 to 55 minutes or until the top is light brown and the center has a slight jiggle to it. Cool on a rack for 2 hours. Cover with plastic wrap and refrigerate for at least 6 hours before decorating or serving.

3. TOPPING: In a small saucepan over low heat, heat sugar and water until sugar melts. Increase heat and boil without stirring until mixture is a rich caramel color. It should take about 8 minutes. Reduce heat to low, add room-temperature cream, stirring constantly to smooth the bubbles. Mix in butter until melted. Add vanilla. Cool slightly. Pour about two-thirds of mixture into center of cake and spread out to edges. Chill cake until caramel is set, about 2 hours.

4. DECORATION: In a well-chilled bowl, whip cream on medium-high speed until soft peaks form. With the mixer still running, sprinkle sugar into cream and continue whipping until firm peaks form. Ice top of cake with whipped cream or pipe a ribbon around border, if desired. Use remaining caramel sauce to garnish each slice of the cheesecake.

Caramel Pecan

CHEESECAKE

Preheat oven to 350°F (180°C)
9-inch (23 cm) cheesecake pan, ungreased, or springform pan
with 3-inch (7.5 cm) sides, greased (for other pan sizes, see page 10)

A *childhood fondness for turtle candies with crunchy pecans wrapped in rich caramel inspired this decadent cheesecake.*

SERVES 10 TO 12

TIP
It's best not to spread the melted caramels right to the edge of the pan. Otherwise, it might stick and make it difficult to remove from the pan.

VARIATION
Pecan lovers will enjoy pecan short-bread cookies in the crust even more than the well-known chocolate sandwich cookies.

CRUST

1 ¼ cups	chocolate sandwich cookie crumbs	300 mL
¼ cup	chopped pecans	50 mL
¼ cup	unsalted butter, melted	50 mL

FILLING

1 cup	caramels	250 mL
2 tbsp	evaporated milk or whipping (35%) cream	25 mL
6 oz	bittersweet chocolate chunks	175 g
2	packages (each 8 oz/250 g) cream cheese, softened	2
1 cup	sour cream	250 mL
½ cup	granulated sugar	125 mL
3	eggs	3
1 tsp	vanilla	5 mL
1 cup	pecans, chopped and toasted	250 mL

1. CRUST: In a medium bowl, combine cookie crumbs, pecans and butter. Press into bottom of cheesecake pan and freeze.

2. FILLING: In a small saucepan over low heat, melt caramels and evaporated milk, stirring frequently, until smooth. Reserve about 3 tbsp (45 mL); cover and refrigerate. (When ready to use, reheat in the microwave or in a small pan over low heat until melted.) Pour remainder over frozen crust, spreading evenly and leaving a ½-inch (1 cm) border uncovered. Sprinkle chocolate chunks over melted caramel. Set aside. In a large mixer bowl, beat cream cheese, sour cream and sugar on medium-high speed for 3 minutes. Add eggs, one at a time, beating after each addition. Mix in vanilla. Fold in pecans. Pour batter over crust. Bake in preheated oven for 45 to 55 minutes or until the top is light brown and the center has a slight jiggle to it. Cool on a rack for 2 hours. Cover with plastic wrap and refrigerate for at least 6 hours before decorating or serving.

3. DECORATION: Drizzle the reserved caramel mixture over top of cake.

Neapolitan

CHEESECAKE

Preheat oven to 350°F (180°C)
9-inch (23 cm) cheesecake pan, ungreased, or springform pan
with 3-inch (7.5 cm) sides, greased (for other pan sizes, see page 10)

As a child Neapolitan ice cream satisfied my love of chocolate and my sister's strawberry craving. But there was always that lonely center of vanilla left untouched in the carton.

SERVES 10 TO 12

TIPS
When shopping for white chocolate make sure cocoa butter is listed as the oil. Try to avoid tropical oils such as palm kernel, cottonseed and coconut oil.

Purchase white chocolate in bars rather than in chip form for this recipe.

VARIATION
Replace strawberries with fresh raspberries when they are in season.

CRUST

1¼ cups	chocolate sandwich cookie crumbs	300 mL
¼ cup	unsalted butter, melted	50 mL

FILLING

3	packages (each 8 oz/250 g) cream cheese, softened	3
¾ cup	granulated sugar	175 mL
3	eggs	3
2 tsp	vanilla	10 mL
2 oz	semi-sweet chocolate, melted and cooled	60 g
2 oz	white chocolate, melted and cooled	60 g
½ cup	fresh strawberries, mashed	125 mL

DECORATION

3 oz	semi-sweet chocolate	90 g
2 tbsp	unsalted butter	25 mL

1. CRUST: In a medium bowl, mix cookie crumbs and butter. Press into bottom of cheesecake pan and freeze.

2. FILLING: In a large mixer bowl, beat cream cheese and sugar on medium-high speed for 3 minutes. Add eggs, one at a time, beating after each addition. Mix in vanilla. Divide batter into three equal portions. Mix the melted semi-sweet chocolate into one-third of batter. Mix the white chocolate into one-third of the batter. Stir strawberries into remaining third. Spread dark chocolate batter over crust. Refrigerate for about 5 minutes to firm. Spread white chocolate batter carefully over dark chocolate layer, covering it completely. Refrigerate for 5 minutes to firm. Spread strawberry portion over white chocolate layer. Bake for 45 to 55 minutes or until the top is light brown and the center has a slight jiggle to it. Cool for 2 hours. Cover and refrigerate for at least 6 hours.

3. DECORATION: In top of double boiler on medium heat with water rippling, whisk chocolate and butter until fully melted. Pour over chilled cake and let drip down the sides. Serve cold.

Austrian

CHEESECAKE

Preheat oven to 350°F (180°C)
9-inch (23 cm) cheesecake pan, ungreased, or springform pan with 3-inch (7.5 cm) sides, greased (for other pan sizes, see page 10)

CRUST

1 cup	all-purpose flour	250 mL
½ tsp	salt	2 mL
2 tsp	packed light brown sugar	10 mL
2 tsp	baking powder	10 mL
¼ cup	unsalted butter, cut into cubes	50 mL
¼ cup	milk	50 mL
1	egg	1

FILLING

2 cups	small curd cottage cheese, drained (see Tip, page 36)	500 mL
½ cup	granulated sugar	125 mL
¾ cup	all-purpose flour	175 mL
5	egg yolks	5
½ cup	milk	125 mL
½ tsp	lemon zest	2 mL
1 tsp	vanilla	5 mL
5	egg whites	5
¼ cup	confectioner's (icing) sugar	50 mL
¼ cup	golden raisins, chopped	50 mL

DECORATION

½ cup	whipping (35%) cream	125 mL
2 tbsp	granulated sugar	25 mL
¼ cup	golden raisins	50 mL

1. CRUST: In a medium bowl, combine flour, salt, brown sugar and baking powder. With a pastry blender or two knives, cut butter into dry mixture until it resembles cornmeal. Add milk and egg, blending into a ball. Press into cheesecake pan. Bake for 10 minutes or until golden brown. Set aside.

2. FILLING: In a large mixer bowl, beat cottage cheese and sugar on medium-high speed for 3 minutes. Mix in flour. Add egg yolks, one at a time, beating after each addition. Stir in milk, zest and vanilla. Set aside. In a clean bowl, whip egg whites until frothy. Sprinkle in confectioner's sugar while you continue to whip egg whites to firm stage. Fold egg whites into cheese mixture. Fold in raisins. Pour over crust. Bake in preheated oven for 55 to 65 minutes or until the top is light brown and the center has a slight jiggle to it. Cool on a rack for 2 hours. Cover with plastic wrap and refrigerate for at least 6 hours before decorating.

3. DECORATION: In a well-chilled mixer bowl, whip cream on medium-high speed until soft peaks form. With the mixer still running, sprinkle sugar into cream and continue whipping until firm peaks form. Ice top of cake with whipped cream or pipe a ribbon around border, if desired. Top with a sprinkling of raisins.

German Quark

German quark cheese is a flavorful soft cheese found in German delis and cheese shops. It's worth the search. You will be delighted with this soft textured cheesecake.

SERVES 10 TO 12

TIP
If you use homemade cookies in the crust, you may not need to use any butter because fresh cookies have more moisture. The crust should feel like wet sand.

VARIATION
Substitute mascarpone cheese if quark cheese is difficult to locate. It's a bit sweeter.

Preheat oven to 325°F (160°C)
9-inch (23 cm) cheesecake pan, ungreased, or springform pan
with 3-inch (7.5 cm) sides, greased (for other pan sizes, see page 10)

CRUST

1½ cups	butter cookie crumbs	375 mL
1 tsp	ground cinnamon	5 mL
¼ cup	unsalted butter, melted	50 mL

FILLING

1 lb	quark cheese	500 g
2 cups	sour cream	500 mL
1 cup	granulated sugar	250 mL
4	egg yolks	4
⅔ cup	all-purpose flour	150 mL
1 tbsp	orange zest	15 mL
¼ cup	fresh orange juice	50 mL
1 tbsp	vanilla	15 mL

DECORATION

	Classic Whipped Cream Topping (see recipe, page 172)	
1 tbsp	orange zest	15 mL

1. CRUST: In a medium bowl, combine crushed cookies, cinnamon and butter. Press into bottom of cheesecake pan and freeze.

2. FILLING: In a large mixer bowl, beat quark, sour cream and sugar on medium-high speed for 3 minutes. Add egg yolks, one at a time, beating after each addition. Mix in flour, zest, orange juice and vanilla. Pour batter over crust. Bake in preheated oven for 65 to 75 minutes or until the top is light brown and the center has a slight jiggle to it. Cool on a rack for 2 hours. Cover with plastic wrap and refrigerate for at least 6 hours before decorating or serving.

3. DECORATION: Ice top of cake with Classic Whipped Cream Topping or pipe a ribbon around border, if desired. Top with a sprinkling of orange zest.

Fresh Fruit Cheesecakes

Almond Blueberry

CHEESECAKE

Wait until you try blueberries in an almond chocolate cheesecake! A new flavor combination to love.

SERVES 10 TO 12

TIPS
You can use frozen blueberries, but don't defrost, just toss berries with about 1 tbsp (15 mL) flour before folding into batter.

Purchase chocolate in bar form rather than chips for the milk chocolate in this recipe.

You can substitute raspberries for the blueberries, if you want.

Preheat oven to 350°F (180°C)
9-inch (23 cm) cheesecake pan, ungreased, or springform pan with 3-inch (7.5 cm) sides, greased (for other pan sizes, see page 10)

CRUST

1 ¼ cups	ground almonds	300 mL
1 ½ tbsp	unsalted butter, melted	22 mL

FILLING

4	packages (each 8 oz/250 g) cream cheese, softened	4
½ cup	unsalted butter, softened	125 mL
⅓ cup	milk	75 mL
3 tbsp	almond liqueur	45 mL
4	eggs	4
1	egg yolk	1
1 lb	milk chocolate, melted and cooled	500 g
1 cup	blueberries	250 mL

DECORATION

2 cups	blueberries	500 mL
3 tbsp	confectioner's (icing) sugar	45 mL

1. CRUST: In a medium bowl, combine almonds and butter. Press into bottom of cheesecake pan and freeze.

2. FILLING: In a large mixer bowl, beat cream cheese and butter on medium-high speed for 3 minutes. Add milk and liqueur. Add eggs and egg yolk, one at a time, beating after each addition. Remove 1 cup (250 mL) batter and stir into melted chocolate. Fold melted chocolate mixture into remaining batter. Fold in 1 cup (250 mL) blueberries. Pour batter into frozen crust. Bake in preheated oven for 45 to 55 minutes or until the top is light brown and the center has a slight jiggle to it. Cool on a rack for 2 hours. Cover with plastic wrap and refrigerate for at least 6 hours before decorating or serving.

3. DECORATING: Place 2 cups (500 mL) berries on top of cake and dust with sugar.

Fresh Cherry

CHEESECAKE

SERVES 10 TO 12

TIP
To freeze cherries in their prime, wash and pit them. Spread out on a cookie sheet. Freeze until hard. Store the hard cherries in plastic freezer bags. Now you can pull them out one at a time rather than in a large mass.

Preheat oven to 350°F (180°C)
9-inch (23 cm) cheesecake pan, ungreased, or springform pan with 3-inch (7.5 cm) sides, greased (for other pan sizes, see page 10)

CRUST

1¼ cups	butter cookie crumbs	300 mL
3 tbsp	unsalted butter, melted	45 mL

FILLING

2	packages (each 8 oz/250 g) cream cheese, softened	2
1 cup	small curd cottage cheese, drained, if necessary (see Tip, page 36)	250 mL
1 cup	sour cream	250 mL
½ cup	all-purpose flour	125 mL
10 oz	sweetened condensed milk	300 mL
3	eggs	3
2 tbsp	fresh lemon juice	25 mL
1 tbsp	vanilla	15 mL
1 tsp	almond extract	5 mL
1 cup	fresh cherries, pitted	250 mL

DECORATION

	Classic Whipped Cream Topping (see recipe, page 172)	
¼ tsp	almond extract	1 mL
12	cherries	12

1. CRUST: In a medium bowl, combine cookie crumbs and butter. Press into bottom of cheesecake pan and freeze.

2. FILLING: In a large mixer bowl, beat cream cheese, cottage cheese, sour cream and flour on medium-high speed for 3 minutes. Mix in sweetened condensed milk. Add eggs, one at a time, beating after each addition. Add lemon juice, vanilla and almond extract. Fold in cherries. Pour batter over frozen crust. Bake in preheated oven for 45 to 55 minutes or until the top is light brown and the center has a slight jiggle to it. Cool for 2 hours. Cover and refrigerate for 6 hours before decorating or serving.

3. DECORATION: Add almond extract to Classic Whipped Cream Topping. Ice top of cake or pipe rosettes around top of cake, if desired. Top with cherries.

Fresh Strawberry Chocolate Chip

CHEESECAKE

SERVES 10 TO 12

TIPS
If the strawberries are not slightly crushed for the batter, you will get large pockets of
liquid from the berries
in the cheesecake.

I use bar chocolate instead of chips and cut into chunks. The chunks melt and make
pockets of chocolate in the cake.

VARIATION
Raspberries or blackberries are a delicious alternative to strawberries.

Preheat oven to 350°F (180°C)
9-inch (23 cm) cheesecake pan, ungreased, or springform pan with 3-inch (7.5 cm) sides, greased (for other pan sizes, see page 10)
13-by 9-inch (3 L) baking pan, lined with parchment

CRUST

1 ¼ cups	chocolate sandwich cookie crumbs	300 mL
3 tbsp	unsalted butter, melted	45 mL

FILLING

4	packages (each 8 oz/250 g) cream cheese, softened	4
1 cup	ricotta cheese, drained	250 mL
¾ cup	sour cream	175 mL
1 ¼ cups	granulated sugar	300 mL
4	eggs	4
2 tbsp	all-purpose flour	25 mL
2 tbsp	fresh lemon juice	25 mL
1 tbsp	vanilla	15 mL
1 cup	strawberries, crushed slightly	250 mL
3 oz	semi-sweet chocolate chunks	90 g

DECORATION

2 cups	strawberries, whole	500 mL
3 oz	semi-sweet chocolate, melted and cooled	90 g

1. CRUST: In a medium bowl, combine cookie crumbs and butter. Press into bottom of cheesecake pan and freeze.

2. FILLING: In a large bowl, beat cream cheese, ricotta, sour cream and sugar on medium-high for 3 minutes. Add eggs, one at a time, beating after each addition. Mix in flour, lemon juice and vanilla. Fold in berries and chocolate chunks. Pour over frozen crust. Bake for 45 to 55 minutes or until the top is light brown. Cool for 2 hours. Cover and refrigerate for 6 hours before decorating.

3. DECORATION: Slice stems from strawberries to create a flat bottom. Dip only the tips of berries in melted chocolate and place flat with tips upward on lined baking pan to dry. When dried, arrange strawberries, tips up, on top of cake.

Tri-Berry
CHESECAKE

I *love berries!*
If there is a fresh
berry on a dessert
menu, I'll choose it
over anything but
chocolate. They are
nature's candies —
packed with flavor
and beauty.

SERVES 10 TO 12

VARIATIONS
Use all of one berry or
two of the varieties if
all three aren't available.

Spread 1 cup (250
mL) berry preserves
on top.

Preheat oven to 350°F (180°C)
9-inch (23 cm) cheesecake pan, ungreased, or springform pan
with 3-inch (7.5 cm) sides, greased (for other pan sizes, see page 10)

CRUST

1 1/4 cups	sugar cookie crumbs	300 mL
3 tbsp	unsalted butter, melted	45 mL

FILLING

4	packages (each 8 oz/250 g) cream cheese, softened	4
1 cup	sour cream	250 mL
1 cup	granulated sugar	250 mL
3	eggs	3
2	egg yolks	2
1/4 cup	all-purpose flour	50 mL
2 1/2 tbsp	fresh lemon juice	32 mL
1 tbsp	vanilla	15 mL
1/2 cup	strawberries, crushed slightly	125 mL
1/2 cup	raspberries, cut into quarters	125 mL
1/2 cup	blackberries, cut into quarters	125 mL

DECORATION

1/2 cup	strawberries, sliced	125 mL
1/2 cup	raspberries, whole	125 mL
1/2 cup	blackberries, whole	125 mL
2 tbsp	port wine	25 mL

1. CRUST: In a medium bowl, combine cookie crumbs and butter. Press into bottom of cheesecake pan and freeze.

2. FILLING: In a large mixer bowl, beat cream cheese, sour cream and sugar on medium-high speed for 3 minutes. Add eggs and yolks, one at a time, beating after each addition. Mix in flour, lemon juice and vanilla. Fold in berries. Pour batter over frozen crust. Bake in preheated oven for 55 to 65 minutes or until the top is light brown and the center has a slight jiggle to it. Cool on a rack for 2 hours. Cover with plastic wrap and refrigerate for at least 6 hours before decorating or serving.

3. DECORATION: In a medium bowl, combine berries and port. Garnish each individual serving piece with a spoonful.

Caramel Apple

CHEESECAKE ❦

Preheat oven to 350°F (180°C)
9-inch (23 cm) cheesecake pan, ungreased, or springform pan
with 3-inch (7.5 cm) sides, greased (for other pan sizes, see page 10)

CRUST

1¼ cups	graham cracker crumbs	300 mL
3 tbsp	unsalted butter, melted	45 mL
1	large baking apple, such as Granny Smith or pippin, sliced into 12 slices	1
6 oz	caramels, cut into quarters	175 g
1 cup	pecans, chopped	250 mL

FILLING

2	packages (each 8 oz/250 g) cream cheese, softened	2
1 cup	granulated sugar	250 mL
3	eggs	3
1 tbsp	ground cinnamon	15 mL
1 tsp	ground nutmeg	5 mL
1 tsp	vanilla	5 mL
½ tsp	lemon zest	2 mL
1 tbsp	fresh lemon juice	15 mL
1 cup	sour cream	250 mL
1	large baking apple, such as Granny Smith or pippin, peeled and sliced into 12 slices	1
¼ cup	pecans, chopped	50 mL

1. **CRUST:** In a medium bowl, combine graham cracker crumbs and butter. Press into bottom of cheesecake pan. Arrange apple slices in a spiral on top of crust. Sprinkle caramels and pecans on top of apples. Bake in preheated oven for 10 minutes. Set on a rack to cool.

2. **FILLING:** In a large mixer bowl, beat cream cheese and sugar on medium-high speed for 3 minutes. Add eggs, one at a time, beating after each addition. Mix in cinnamon, nutmeg, vanilla, lemon zest and lemon juice. Fold in sour cream. Pour batter over crust. Arrange sliced apples and pecans on top of batter. Bake in preheated oven for 45 to 55 minutes or until the top is light brown and the center has a slight jiggle to it. Cool on a rack for 2 hours. Cover with plastic wrap and refrigerate for at least 6 hours before serving.

Crisp Apple

CHEESECAKE

SERVES 10 TO 12

TIP
In a small bowl, mix 1 tbsp (15 mL) vinegar or lemon juice in cold water and store the prepared apple slices until ready to toss with spices. This will prevent them from discoloring.

VARIATION
Pecan shortbread cookie crumbs are a delicious crust alternate to graham cracker crumbs. They also combine well with crisp apple flavors.

Preheat oven to 350°F (180°C)
9-inch (23 cm) cheesecake pan, ungreased, or springform pan with 3-inch (7.5 cm) sides, greased (for other pan sizes, see page 10)

CRUST

1 1/4 cups	graham cracker crumbs	300 mL
3 tbsp	unsalted butter, melted	45 mL

FILLING

4	packages (each 8 oz/250 g) cream cheese, softened	4
1 1/4 cups	packed light brown sugar	300 mL
4	eggs	4
1 tbsp	vanilla	15 mL
1 tsp	fresh lemon juice	5 mL

TOPPING

1/4 cup	granulated sugar	50 mL
1/2 tsp	ground cinnamon	2 mL
1/4 tsp	ground cloves	1 mL
2 tbsp	packed light brown sugar	25 mL
1/4 cup	all-purpose flour	50 mL
1 cup	thinly sliced peeled apples (see Tip, left)	250 mL

1. CRUST: In a medium bowl, mix graham cracker crumbs and butter. Press into bottom of cheesecake pan and freeze.

2. FILLING: In a large mixer bowl, beat cream cheese and brown sugar on medium-high speed for 3 minutes. Add eggs, one at a time, beating after each addition. Mix in vanilla and lemon juice. Pour over frozen crust.

3. TOPPING: Combine sugar, cinnamon, cloves, brown sugar and flour. Toss apple slices with sugar mixture. Arrange slices decoratively on top of batter. Bake in preheated oven for 45 to 55 minutes or until the top is light brown and the center has a slight jiggle to it. Cool on a rack for 2 hours. Cover with plastic wrap and refrigerate for at least 6 hours before serving.

French Apple

CHEESECAKE

Preheat oven to 350°F (180°C)
9-inch (23 cm) cheesecake pan, ungreased, or springform pan
with 3-inch (7.5 cm) sides, greased (for other pan sizes, see page 10)

This cheesecake is rich with fresh apples and a topping just like a French apple pie.

SERVES 10 TO 12

TIP
You can prepare this cheesecake and freeze, including the topping, up to 3 weeks prior to serving. To freeze, I keep my cheesecakes in the pan and cover with plastic wrap, then foil. To use, place the wrapped cheesecake into the refrigerator a day prior to use.

CRUST

1 ¼ cups	graham cracker crumbs	300 mL
3 tbsp	unsalted butter, melted	45 mL

FILLING

3	packages (each 8 oz/250 g) cream cheese, softened	3
1 cup	sour cream	250 mL
1 cup	packed light brown sugar	250 mL
¼ cup	liquid honey	50 mL
4	eggs	4
1 tbsp	vanilla	15 mL
1 tsp	fresh lemon juice	5 mL
1 tsp	ground cinnamon	5 mL
½ tsp	fresh ground nutmeg	2 mL
¼ tsp	ground cloves	1 mL

TOPPING

3 tbsp	unsalted butter, cold, cut into cubes	45 mL
¼ cup	all-purpose flour	50 mL
¼ cup	packed light brown sugar	50 mL
½ tsp	ground cinnamon	2 mL
¼ tsp	ground cloves	1 mL
1	medium baking apple, such as Granny Smith or Pippin, peeled and sliced into 12 thin slices	1

DECORATION

½ cup	confectioner's (icing) sugar	125 mL
2 tbsp	unsalted butter, melted	25 mL
2 tbsp	hot water	25 mL

VARIATION
Use the topping in the filling of the cheesecake instead of the top. Just blend it into the batter and bake as directed.

1. CRUST: In a medium bowl, combine graham cracker crumbs and butter. Press into bottom of cheesecake pan and freeze.

2. FILLING: In a large mixer bowl, beat cream cheese, sour cream, brown sugar and honey on medium-high speed for 3 minutes. Add eggs, one at a time, beating after each addition. Mix in vanilla and lemon juice. Beat in cinnamon, nutmeg and cloves. Pour over frozen crust.

3. TOPPING: In a medium bowl, using a pastry blender or two knives, cut butter into flour as if making a piecrust. Add brown sugar, cinnamon and cloves. Toss apples with this mixture. Arrange apple mixture in a spiral over batter. Bake in preheated oven for 60 to 75 minutes or until apples are light brown and slightly firm in the center. Cool on a rack for 2 hours. Cover with plastic wrap and refrigerate at least 6 hours before decorating or serving.

4. DECORATION: In a small bowl, whisk sugar with butter and hot water. Drizzle on top of chilled cake.

Kiwi

CHEESECAKE

Refreshing with the light sweetness of kiwi and no crust, this cheesecake is perfect for a summer day with a glass of limeade.

SERVES 10 TO 12

TIPS

When purchasing fresh kiwis they should be firm like a ripe tomato.

Use fresh lime juice. Bottled lime juice can have a metallic taste.

Preheat oven to 350°F (180°C)

9-inch (23 cm) cheesecake or springform pan with 3-inch (7.5 cm) sides, lined with parchment (for other pan sizes, see page 10)

FILLING

2	packages (each 8 oz/250 g) cream cheese, softened	2
2 cups	ricotta cheese, drained (see Tip, page 25)	500 mL
1 cup	sour cream	250 mL
1½ cups	granulated sugar	375 mL
5	eggs	5
3	medium kiwis, peeled and puréed	3
½ cup	all-purpose flour	125 mL
2 tbsp	fresh lime juice	25 mL
1 tbsp	vanilla	15 mL

DECORATION

3	medium kiwis, peeled and sliced thin	3
½ cup	apricot preserves	125 mL

1. FILLING: In a large mixer bowl, beat cream cheese, ricotta, sour cream and sugar on medium-high speed for 3 minutes. Add eggs, one at a time, beating after each addition. Stir in kiwi purée, flour, lime juice and vanilla. Pour into prepared cheesecake pan. Bake in preheated oven for 55 to 65 minutes or until the top is light brown and the center has a slight jiggle to it. Cool on a rack for 2 hours. Cover with plastic wrap and refrigerate for at least 6 hours before decorating.

2. DECORATION: Place sliced kiwis on top of cake. In a small saucepan, bring apricot preserves to medium heat. Press through a sieve. Brush on top of kiwis. This will keep the fruit looking fresh.

Peaches and Cream

CHEESECAKE

> This cheesecake is perfect for the spring holidays with its fresh peaches and creamy base.

SERVES 10 TO 12

TIP
Use ripe peaches in season. To ripen any stone fruit, such as peaches or nectarines, place in a brown paper bag for a few days until soft when lightly touched.

VARIATION
Try almonds or walnuts in place of pecans.

Preheat oven to 350°F (180°C)
9-inch (23 cm) cheesecake pan, ungreased, or springform pan with 3-inch (7.5 cm) sides, greased (for other pan sizes, see page 10)

CRUST

1 1/4 cups	graham cracker crumbs	300 mL
1/4 cup	pecans, toasted and ground	50 mL
3 tbsp	unsalted butter, melted	45 mL

FILLING

4	packages (each 8 oz/250 g) cream cheese, softened	4
1 cup	whipping (35%) cream	250 mL
1 cup	granulated sugar	250 mL
4	eggs	4
1/4 cup	all-purpose flour	50 mL
2 tsp	vanilla	10 mL
2	medium peaches, peeled and sliced	2
1/4 cup	pecans, chopped	50 mL

DECORATION

	Classic Whipped Cream Topping (see recipe, page 172)	
1	medium peach, peeled and sliced	1

1. CRUST: In a bowl, combine graham cracker crumbs, pecans and butter. Press into cheesecake pan and freeze.

2. FILLING: In a large mixer bowl, beat cream cheese, whipping cream and sugar on medium-high speed for 3 minutes. Add eggs, one at a time, beating after each addition. Stir in flour and vanilla. Pour half of batter into frozen crust. Place peach slices on top of batter, then sprinkle pecans on top. Pour remaining batter over peaches. Bake in preheated oven for 45 to 55 minutes or until the top is light brown and the center has a slight jiggle to it. Cool on a rack for 2 hours. Cover with plastic wrap and refrigerate for at least 6 hours before decorating or serving.

3. DECORATION: Ice top of cake with Classic Whipped Cream Topping or pipe rosettes around top of cake, if desired. Top with peach slices.

Maui Tropical

CHEESECAKE ❧

Tropical fruit from the islands make this cheesecake feel like a friendly aloha!

SERVES 10 TO 12

TIP
A non-alcoholic substitute for rum is orange juice concentrate.

VARIATIONS
You can substitute mango or kiwi if papaya is not available.

Preheat oven to 350°F (180°C)
9-inch (23 cm) cheesecake pan, ungreased, or springform pan
with 3-inch (7.5 cm) sides, greased (for other pan sizes, see page 10)

CRUST

1½ cups	macadamia nuts, toasted and coarsely ground	375 mL
1 tbsp	all-purpose flour	15 mL
¼ cup	granulated sugar	50 mL

FILLING

4	packages (each 8 oz/250 g) cream cheese, softened	4
1½ cups	granulated sugar	375 mL
4	eggs	4
½ cup	well-drained crushed pineapple, about 8 oz (227 mL) can	125 mL
½ cup	finely chopped papaya, about ½ medium papaya	125 mL
1 tbsp	rum	15 mL
2 tsp	vanilla	10 mL

DECORATION

5 to 6	pineapple slices, about 6 oz (175 mL) can	5 to 6
5 to 6	papaya slices, about ½ medium papaya	5 to 6

1. CRUST: In a medium bowl, combine nuts, flour and sugar. Press firmly into bottom of cheesecake pan. Set aside.

2. FILLING: In a large mixer bowl, beat cream cheese and sugar on medium speed for 3 minutes. Add eggs, one at a time, beating after each addition. Stir in pineapple, papaya, rum and vanilla. Pour batter over crust. Bake in preheated oven for 45 to 55 minutes or until the top is light brown and the center has a slight jiggle to it. Cool on a rack for 2 hours. Cover with plastic wrap and refrigerate for at least 6 hours before decorating or serving.

3. DECORATION: Alternate pineapple and papaya slices on top. Chill until ready to serve.

Piña Colada

CHEESECAKE

Preheat oven to 350°F (180°C)
9-inch (23 cm) cheesecake pan, ungreased, or springform pan
with 3-inch (7.5 cm) sides, greased (for other pan sizes, see page 10)

Cheesecake with an island twist! You can serve this with a rum punch as a dessert to a luau.

SERVES 10 TO 12

TIP
Coconut is often burned by a pastry chef. To avoid crying over burnt coconut, follow this technique. Spread coconut in a single layer on a cookie sheet. Bake in a preheated 350°F (180°C) oven for 3 minutes. Check the coconut and stir. Set the timer for another 3 minutes. Repeat until coconut is lightly browned.

VARIATION
Add 1 tbsp (15 mL) rum to the cheese-cake when you add vanilla for a little kick.

CRUST

1 1/4 cups	graham cracker crumbs	300 mL
1/2 cup	flaked coconut	125 mL
3 tbsp	unsalted butter, melted	45 mL

FILLING

1	can (20 oz/540 mL) pineapple, diced	1
3 tbsp	packed light brown sugar	45 mL
4	packages (each 8 oz/250 g) cream cheese, softened	4
1 1/4 cups	granulated sugar	300 mL
1/4 cup	all-purpose flour	50 mL
4	eggs	4
1/2 cup	coconut milk	125 mL
2 tsp	vanilla	10 mL

DECORATION

	Classic Whipped Cream Topping (see recipe, page 172)	
1/4 cup	flaked coconut, toasted (see Tip, left)	50 mL

1. **CRUST:** In a bowl, combine graham cracker crumbs, coconut and butter. Press into cheesecake pan and freeze.

2. **FILLING:** In a saucepan on medium heat, cook pineapple and brown sugar until soft and syrupy, about 3 minutes. Let sit for 10 minutes, then drain, discarding syrup. In a large bowl, beat cream cheese, sugar and flour on medium-high for 3 minutes. Add eggs, one at a time, beating after each addition. Mix in coconut milk and vanilla. Pour half of batter into frozen crust. Arrange the pineapple mixture on top. Pour remaining batter over pineapple mixture. Bake for 45 to 55 minutes or until the top is light brown. Cool for 2 hours. Cover with plastic wrap and refrigerate for 6 hours before decorating or serving.

3. **DECORATION:** Ice top of cake with Classic Whipped Cream Topping or pipe a ribbon around sides of cake, if desired. Sprinkle with toasted coconut.

Roasted Banana Rum

CHEESECAKE

An island treat!
Roasted bananas are
simple to make on
the barbecue or in
the oven.

SERVES 10 TO 12

TIP
You can also barbecue
the bananas. Preheat
grill to medium and
spray the rack so the
peels do not stick.
You can roast the
bananas, peel them
and then freeze for
future use.

VARIATION
Substitute apple
juice for rum.

Preheat broiler
9-inch (23 cm) cheesecake pan, ungreased, or springform pan
with 3-inch (7.5 cm) sides, greased (for other pan sizes, see page 10)

CRUST

1 1/4 cups	butter cookie crumbs	300 mL
1/4 cup	pecans, toasted and ground	50 mL
3 tbsp	unsalted butter, melted	45 mL

FILLING

3	medium bananas, firm	3
1/2 cup	light rum	125 mL
4	packages (each 8 oz/250 g) cream cheese, softened	4
1 1/4 cups	granulated sugar	300 mL
1/2 cup	sour cream	125 mL
1/4 cup	liquid honey	50 mL
4	eggs	4
1 tbsp	vanilla	15 mL
1 tsp	ground cinnamon	5 mL
1/2 tsp	ground cloves	2 mL
1/2 cup	pecans, toasted and chopped	125 mL

DECORATION

	Classic Whipped Cream Topping (see recipe, page 172)	
12	dried banana chips	12

1. CRUST: In a medium bowl, combine cookie crumbs, pecans and butter. Press into bottom of cheesecake pan and freeze.

2. FILLING: With oven on broil, place unpeeled bananas in a single layer on a baking pan. Roast about 5 minutes per side or until peel darkens. Let cool. Peel and place into a bowl with rum. Smash with a fork. Set aside. In a large mixer bowl, beat cream cheese and sugar on medium-high for 3 minutes. Add sour cream and honey. Add eggs, one at a time, beating after each addition. Mix in vanilla, cinnamon and cloves. Pour half of batter into crust. Spread rum mixture on top and sprinkle with pecans. Pour on remaining batter. Bake in 350°F (180°C) preheated oven for 45 to 55 minutes or until the top is light brown. Cool for 2 hours. Cover and refrigerate for 6 hours before decorating or serving.

3. DECORATION: Ice top of cake with whipped cream or pipe rosettes around top of cake. Top with banana chips.

Banana Nut

CHESECAKE

SERVES 10 TO 12

TIP
Look for dried bananas in the health food section of your supermarket. Do not use fresh bananas for decorating because they will turn black before you can serve the dessert.

VARIATION
Try almonds or walnuts instead of pecans.

Preheat oven to 350°F (180°C)
9-inch (23 cm) cheesecake pan, ungreased, or springform pan with 3-inch (7.5 cm) sides, greased (for other pan sizes, see page 10)

CRUST

1¼ cup	graham cracker crumbs	300 mL
¼ cup	pecans, toasted and ground	50 mL
3 tbsp	unsalted butter, melted	45 mL

FILLING

3	packages (each 8 oz/250 g) cream cheese, softened	3
1 cup	sour cream	250 mL
1¼ cups	mashed ripe bananas, about 3 large	300 mL
¼ cup	all-purpose flour	50 mL
1 cup	granulated sugar	250 mL
3	eggs	3
½ cup	pecans, toasted and ground	125 mL
3 tsp	ground cinnamon	15 mL
1 tsp	ground nutmeg	5 mL
1 tsp	vanilla	5 mL

DECORATION

	Classic Whipped Cream Topping (see recipe, page 172)	
12	dried banana chips	12

1. CRUST: In a bowl, combine graham cracker crumbs, pecans and butter. Press into cheesecake pan and freeze.

2. FILLING: In a large mixer bowl, beat cream cheese, sour cream, bananas, flour and sugar on medium-high speed for 3 minutes. Add eggs, one at a time, beating after each addition. Fold in pecans, cinnamon, nutmeg and vanilla. Pour batter over frozen crust. Bake in preheated oven for 45 to 55 minutes or until the top is light brown and the center has a slight jiggle to it. Cool on a rack for 2 hours. Cover with plastic wrap and refrigerate for at least 6 hours before decorating or serving.

3. DECORATION: Ice top of cake with Classic Whipped Cream Topping or pipe rosettes around top of cake, if desired. Top with dried banana chips.

Poached Pear

CHEESECAKE

SERVES 10 TO 12

TIPS

A Dutch oven is a large pot that can go from stovetop to oven. You can poach the pears up to 3 days prior to use.

When measuring honey, lightly spray the measuring cup with a nonstick spray, so the honey will release easily.

Preheat oven to 350°F (180°C)
9-inch (23 cm) cheesecake pan, ungreased, or springform pan with 3-inch (7.5 cm) sides, greased (for other pan sizes, see page 10)
4-quart (4 L) Dutch oven

CRUST

1¼ cups	graham cracker crumbs	300 mL
¼ cup	pecans, toasted and ground	50 mL
3 tbsp	unsalted butter, melted	45 mL

FILLING

2½ cups	white Zinfandel wine	625 mL
2 tbsp	granulated sugar	25 mL
¼ tsp	ground cloves	1 mL
½ tsp	ground cinnamon	2 mL
6	medium ripe pears, peeled, halved and cored, about 1½ lbs (675 g)	6
3	packages (each 8 oz/250 g) cream cheese, softened	3
1 cup	granulated sugar	250 mL
¼ cup	liquid honey	50 mL
4	eggs	4
1 tbsp	vanilla	15 mL
1 tsp	ground cinnamon	5 mL
½ tsp	ground cloves	2 mL
½ cup	pecans, toasted and chopped	125 mL

DECORATION

½ cup	whipping (35%) cream	125 mL
2 tbsp	granulated sugar	25 mL

VARIATION
Substitute apple juice
for Zinfandel wine.

1. CRUST: In a medium bowl, combine graham cracker crumbs, pecans and butter. Press into bottom of cheesecake pan and freeze.

2. FILLING: In a large Dutch oven, place wine, sugar, cloves and cinnamon. Cook on medium heat, covered, until it starts to boil, about 4 minutes. Add pears and simmer until pears are fork tender but not too soft. Thinly slice pears and set aside. In a large mixer bowl, beat cream cheese and sugar on medium-high speed for 3 minutes. Add honey. Add eggs, one at a time, beating after each addition. Mix in vanilla, cinnamon and cloves. Pour half of batter into frozen crust. Arrange half of pears on top of batter, reserving other half for decoration. Sprinkle pecans over pears. Pour remaining batter over pears. Bake in preheated oven for 45 to 55 minutes or until the top is light brown and the center has a slight jiggle to it. Cool on a rack for 2 hours. Cover with plastic wrap and refrigerate for at least 6 hours before decorating or serving.

3. DECORATION: In a well-chilled bowl, whip cream on medium-high speed until soft peaks form. With the mixer still running, sprinkle sugar into cream and continue whipping until firm peaks form. Ice top of cake or pipe a border around cake, if desired. Arrange remaining pear slices in a spiral around top of cake.

Apricot Hazelnut

C H E E S E C A K E

SERVES 10 TO 12

TIPS
Process almonds and flour together in a food processor to avoid making almond butter.

To remove peel from fruit quickly, place an "x" in the bottom with
a small knife, piercing only the skin. Place fruit in rapidly boiling water for about 30 seconds. Cool in cold water.
The peel should remove easily.

Preheat oven to 350°F (180°C)
9-inch (23 cm) cheesecake pan, ungreased, or springform pan
with 3-inch (7.5 cm) sides, greased (for other pan sizes, see page 10)

CRUST

1 ¼ cups	ground almonds (see Tip, left)	300 mL
¼ cup	all-purpose flour	50 mL
3 tbsp	unsalted butter, melted	45 mL

FILLING

4	packages (each 8 oz/250 g) cream cheese, softened	4
1 cup	whipping (35%) cream	250 mL
1 cup	granulated sugar	250 mL
¼ cup	all-purpose flour	50 mL
4	eggs	4
3 tbsp	hazelnut liqueur	45 mL
2 tsp	vanilla	10 mL
4	medium apricots, peeled, pitted and sliced, about 1 lb (500 g)	4
¼ cup	chopped almonds	50 mL

DECORATION

	Classic Whipped Cream Topping (see recipe, page 172)	
2	medium apricots, peeled, pitted and sliced, about ½ lb (250 g)	2

1. CRUST: In a medium bowl, combine almonds, flour and butter. Press into bottom of cheesecake pan and freeze.

2. FILLING: In a large mixer bowl, beat cream cheese, whipping cream, sugar and flour on medium-high speed for 3 minutes. Add eggs, one at a time, beating after each addition. Mix in hazelnut liqueur and vanilla. Pour half of batter over frozen crust. Arrange apricot slices on top of batter and sprinkle almonds on top. Pour remaining batter over apricots. Bake in preheated oven for 45 to 55 minutes or until the top is light brown and the center has a slight jiggle to it. Cool on a rack for 2 hours. Cover with plastic wrap and refrigerate for at least 6 hours before decorating or serving.

3. DECORATION: Ice top of cake with Classic Whipped Cream Topping or pipe rosettes around top of cake, if desired. Top with apricot slices.

Chocolate Cheesecakes

German Chocolate Cheesecake (page 74)

Overleaf: Chocolate Espresso Swirl Cheesecake (page 70)

Black Forest

CHEESECAKE

SERVES 10 TO 12

TIP
Make sure the melted chocolate has cooled slightly before adding or the cake will have chocolate chunks in the batter.

VARIATION
Fresh cherries, cut in half and placed cut-side down on top of cheesecake, is a stunning visual and taste sensation.

Preheat oven to 350°F (180°C)
9-inch (23 cm) cheesecake pan, ungreased, or springform pan
with 3-inch (7.5 cm) sides, greased (for other pan sizes, see page 10)

CRUST

1¼ cups	chocolate sandwich cookie crumbs	300 mL
3 tbsp	unsalted butter, melted	45 mL

FILLING

2	packages (each 8 oz/250 g) cream cheese, softened	2
⅔ cup	granulated sugar	150 mL
2	eggs	2
1 tsp	vanilla	5 mL
6 oz	semi-sweet chocolate, melted and cooled	175 g

DECORATION

½ cup	whipping (35%) cream	125 mL
2 tbsp	granulated sugar	25 mL
1	can (21 oz/645 mL) cherry pie filling	1

1. CRUST: In a medium bowl, combine cookie crumbs and butter. Press into bottom of cheesecake pan and freeze.

2. FILLING: In a large mixer bowl, beat cream cheese and sugar on medium-high speed for 3 minutes. Add eggs, one at a time, beating after each addition. Mix in vanilla and melted chocolate. Pour batter over frozen crust. Bake in preheated oven for 45 to 55 minutes or until the top is light brown and the center has a slight jiggle to it. Cool on a rack for 2 hours. Cover with plastic wrap and refrigerate for at least 6 hours before decorating or serving.

3. DECORATION: In a well-chilled bowl, whip cream on medium-high speed until soft peaks form. With the mixer still running, sprinkle sugar into cream and continue whipping until firm peaks form. Pipe a border around the edge of cake, if desired. Fill center with cherry pie filling.

Chocolate Caramel Pecan

CHESECAKE 🌾

Preheat oven to 350°F (180°C)
9-inch (23 cm) cheesecake pan, ungreased, or springform pan
with 3-inch (7.5 cm) sides, greased (for other pan sizes, see page 10)

Y *ou only need to serve very thin slices of this dark, rich cheesecake as the intensity of the chocolate, caramel and pecans is almost intoxicating.*

🌾

SERVES 14 TO 16

TIPS
Coarsely chop a chocolate bar in chunks instead of using chips.

It's best not to spread the melted caramels right to the edge of the pan. Otherwise, it might stick and make it difficult to remove from the pan.

VARIATION
Dust unsweetened cocoa powder on top and around the edge of the serving plate.

CRUST

1 ¼ cups	chocolate sandwich cookie crumbs	300 mL
¼ cup	unsalted butter, melted	50 mL

FILLING

1 cup	caramels	250 mL
2 tbsp	evaporated milk or whipping (35%) cream	25 mL
6 oz	bittersweet chocolate chunks	175 g
2	packages (each 8 oz/250 g) cream cheese, softened	2
1 cup	sour cream	250 mL
½ cup	granulated sugar	125 mL
¼ cup	unsweetened cocoa powder, sifted	50 mL
3	eggs	3
1 tsp	vanilla	5 mL
1 cup	pecans, toasted and chopped	250 mL

1. CRUST: In a medium bowl, combine cookie crumbs and butter. Press into bottom of cheesecake pan and freeze.

2. FILLING: In a small saucepan over low heat, melt caramels with evaporated milk, stirring often, until smooth. Reserve 3 tbsp (45 mL) for decorating; cover and refrigerate. (When ready to use, reheat in the microwave.) Pour remaining caramel mixture over frozen crust, spreading evenly and leaving a ½-inch (1 cm) border uncovered. Sprinkle chocolate chunks over caramel. Set aside. In a large bowl, beat cream cheese, sour cream, sugar and cocoa powder on medium-high speed for 3 minutes. Add eggs, one at a time, beating after each addition. Mix in vanilla. Fold in pecans. Pour over chocolate and caramel. Bake in preheated oven for 40 to 50 minutes or until the top is light brown and the center has a slight jiggle to it. Cool for 2 hours. Cover with plastic wrap and refrigerate for 6 hours before decorating or serving.

3. DECORATION: Drizzle reserved caramel mixture over cake.

Chocolate Cherry
CHEESECAKE

Chocolate chunk cheesecake topped with cherries is a showstopper of a dessert!

SERVES 10 TO 12

TIP
To make chocolate chunks, take a good-quality chocolate bar and cut into big chunks with a knife.

VARIATION
Use white chocolate chunks instead of the semi-sweet chocolate.

Preheat oven to 350°F (180°C)
9-inch (23 cm) cheesecake pan, ungreased, or springform pan with 3-inch (7.5 cm) sides, greased (for other pan sizes, see page 10)

CRUST

1 ¼ cups	chocolate sandwich cookies crumbs	300 mL
3 tbsp	unsalted butter, melted	45 mL

FILLING

3	packages (each 8 oz/250 g) cream cheese, softened	3
1 cup	granulated sugar	250 mL
3	eggs	3
1	egg yolk	1
2 tsp	vanilla	10 mL
6 oz	semi-sweet chocolate chunks	175 g

DECORATION

½ cup	whipping (35%) cream	125 mL
2 tbsp	granulated sugar	25 mL
1	can (21 oz/645 mL) cherry pie filling	1

1. CRUST: In a medium bowl, combine cookie crumbs and butter. Press into bottom of cheesecake pan and freeze.

2. FILLING: In a large mixer bowl, beat cream cheese and sugar on medium-high speed for 3 minutes. Add eggs and egg yolk, one at a time, beating after each addition. Add vanilla and chocolate chunks. Pour batter over frozen crust. Bake in preheated oven for 45 to 55 minutes or until the top is light brown and the center has a slight jiggle to it. Cool on a rack for 2 hours. Cover with plastic wrap and refrigerate for at least 6 hours before decorating or serving.

3. DECORATION: In a well-chilled bowl, whip cream on medium-high speed until soft peaks form. With the mixer still running, sprinkle sugar into cream and continue whipping until firm peaks form. Pipe a border around the edge of cake, if desired. Fill center with cherry pie filling.

Chocolate Chunk Peanut Butter

CHEESECAKE

With its chocolate and peanut butter combination, this cheesecake is just like a candy bar.

SERVES 10 TO 12

TIP
Use a commercial creamy peanut butter. The natural peanut butters have too much oil for this recipe.

VARIATION
If you think you can handle more chocolate, replace the peanut butter cookie crumbs with chocolate sandwich cookies and omit flour.

Preheat oven to 350°F (180°C)
9-inch (23 cm) cheesecake pan, ungreased, or springform pan with 3-inch (7.5 cm) sides, greased (for other pan sizes, see page 10)

CRUST

1¼ cups	peanut butter sandwich cookie crumbs	300 mL
¼ cup	all-purpose flour	50 mL
¼ cup	unsalted butter, melted	50 mL

FILLING

4	packages (each 8 oz/250 g) cream cheese, softened	4
1¼ cups	granulated sugar	300 mL
4	eggs	4
1 cup	peanut butter, creamy style	250 mL
3 tbsp	fresh lemon juice	45 mL
1 tsp	vanilla	5 mL
2 cups	semi-sweet chocolate chunks	500 mL

TOPPING

½ cup	sour cream	125 mL
¼ cup	granulated sugar	50 mL
¼ cup	peanut butter, creamy style	50 mL
1 tbsp	fresh lemon juice	15 mL
½ tsp	vanilla	2 mL
½ cup	chocolate chunks	125 mL

1. CRUST: In a medium bowl, combine cookie crumbs, flour and butter. Press into bottom of cheesecake pan and freeze.

2. FILLING: In a large mixer bowl, beat cream cheese and sugar on medium-high for 3 minutes. Add eggs, one at a time, beating after each addition. Stir in peanut butter. Mix in lemon juice and vanilla. Fold in chocolate chunks. Pour into frozen crust. Bake for 45 to 55 minutes or until the top is light brown. Cool on the counter for 10 minutes (do not turn the oven off). The cake will sink slightly.

3. TOPPING: In a bowl, combine sour cream, sugar, peanut butter, lemon juice and vanilla. Pour into center of cake and spread to edges. Sprinkle with chocolate. Bake for 5 minutes more. Cool for 2 hours. Cover and refrigerate for 6 hours.

CHOCOLATE CHEESECAKES **69**

Chocolate Espresso Swirl

CHEESECAKE ✒

SERVES 10 TO 12

TIP
Cool melted chocolate to room temperature before adding the cheesecake batter or the chocolate will stiffen up and you will have to start all over.

Preheat oven to 350°F (180°C)
9-inch (23 cm) cheesecake pan, ungreased, or springform pan with 3-inch (7.5 cm) sides, greased (for other pan sizes, see page 10)

CRUST

1 ½ cups	chocolate sandwich cookie crumbs	375 mL
¼ cup	unsalted butter, melted	50 mL

FILLING

4	packages (each 8 oz/250 g) cream cheese, softened	4
1 ½ cups	granulated sugar	375 mL
½ cup	sour cream	125 mL
4	eggs	4
1 tbsp	instant coffee powder	15 mL
1 tbsp	hot water	15 mL
1 tsp	vanilla	5 mL
3 oz	bittersweet chocolate, melted and cooled	90 g

DECORATION

½ cup	whipping (35%) cream	125 mL
2 tbsp	granulated sugar	25 mL
12	mocha candy coffee beans	12

VARIATION
Add 2 tbsp (25 mL)
rum or coffee liqueur
for a little kick.

1. CRUST: In a medium bowl, combine cookie crumbs and butter. Press into bottom of cheesecake pan and freeze.

2. FILLING: In a large mixer bowl, beat cream cheese and sugar on medium-high speed for 3 minutes. Add sour cream. Add eggs, one at a time, beating after each addition. In a small bowl, dissolve coffee powder in hot water. While the mixer is running, pour coffee in a steady stream into the batter. Add vanilla. Stir 1 cup (250 mL) batter into melted chocolate and set aside. Pour remaining batter over frozen crust.

3. Using a spoon, drop six large puddles of melted chocolate mixture on top of batter. Using a small knife drag through the puddles in spiral motions to create a marbling effect. Bake in preheated oven for 45 to 55 minutes or until the top is light brown and the center has a slight jiggle to it. Cool on a rack for 2 hours. Cover with plastic wrap and refrigerate for at least 6 hours before decorating or serving.

4. DECORATION: In a well-chilled bowl, whip cream on medium-high speed until soft peaks form. With the mixer still running, sprinkle sugar into cream and continue whipping until firm peaks form. Ice top of cake with whipped cream or pipe rosettes around top of cake, if desired. Top with mocha coffee beans.

Chocolate Truffle

CHEESECAKE ❧

SERVES 10 TO 12

TIP
You can prepare the chocolate cream mixture up to 3 days prior to use.

VARIATION
You can add 2 tablespoons (25 mL) Chambord raspberry liqueur and ¼ cup (50 mL) fresh raspberries to make Raspberry Chocolate Truffle Cheesecake.

Preheat oven to 350°F (180°C)
9-inch (23 cm) cheesecake pan, ungreased, or springform pan with 3-inch (7.5 cm) sides, greased (for other pan sizes, see page 10)

CRUST

1½ cups	chocolate sandwich cookie crumbs	375 mL
¼ cup	unsalted butter, melted	50 mL

FILLING

½ cup	whipping (35%) cream	125 mL
8 oz	bittersweet chocolate, chopped fine	250 g
3	packages (each 8 oz/250 g) cream cheese, softened	3
1 cup	granulated sugar	250 mL
2	eggs	2
¼ cup	unsweetened cocoa powder	50 mL
1 tbsp	all-purpose flour	15 mL
½ cup	sour cream	125 mL
1 tsp	vanilla	5 mL

DECORATION

	Classic Whipped Cream Topping (see recipe, page 172)	
½ cup	chocolate shavings	125 mL

1. CRUST: In a medium bowl, mix cookie crumbs and butter. Press into bottom of cheesecake pan and freeze.

2. FILLING: In a small saucepan over high heat, bring cream to a boil. Pour over chocolate in a bowl and stir until blended. Set aside in the freezer until very firm. In a large bowl, beat cream cheese and sugar on medium-high for 3 minutes. Add eggs, one at a time, beating after each addition. Add cocoa powder, flour, sour cream and vanilla. Using a spoon, scrape firm chocolate mixture into small pieces and fold into batter. Pour over frozen crust. Bake for 45 to 55 minutes or until the top is light brown. Cool on a rack for 2 hours. Cover and refrigerate for 6 hours before decorating.

3. DECORATION: Ice top of cake with Classic Whipped Cream Topping or pipe rosettes around top of cake, if desired. Top with chocolate shavings.

Coffee-Flavored Brownie

CHEESECAKE

SERVES 10 TO 12

TIP
A second large mixer bowl saves washing dishes mid-recipe.

VARIATION
Ice the cheesecake with cherry pie filling or Fresh Raspberry Sauce (see recipe, page 174).

Preheat oven to 350°F (180°C)
9-inch (23 cm) cheesecake or springform pan with 3-inch (7.5 cm) sides, lined with parchment paper (for other pan sizes, see page 10)

BASE

1 cup	unsalted butter, softened	250 mL
1 cup	granulated sugar	250 mL
4	eggs	4
2 tbsp	coffee-flavored liqueur	25 mL
2 tsp	vanilla	10 mL
½ tsp	salt	2 mL
1 lb	semi-sweet chocolate, melted and cooled	500 g
1 cup	all-purpose flour	250 mL

FILLING

2	packages (each 8 oz/250 g) cream cheese, softened	2
¾ cup	granulated sugar	175 mL
4	eggs	4
2 tbsp	all-purpose flour	25 mL
¼ cup	sour cream	50 mL
2 tsp	vanilla	10 mL

1. BASE: In a large mixer bowl, beat butter and sugar on medium-high speed for 3 minutes. Add eggs, one at a time, beating after each addition. Mix in liqueur, vanilla, salt and chocolate. Quickly beat in flour. Smooth into prepared cheesecake pan. Refrigerate for 3 minutes.

2. FILLING: In a large mixer bowl, beat cream cheese and sugar on medium-high speed for 3 minutes. Add eggs, one at a time, beating after each addition. Mix in flour, sour cream and vanilla. Spread batter evenly over top of brownie layer. Bake in preheated oven for 40 to 50 minutes or until the top is light brown and the center has a slight jiggle to it. Cool on a rack for 2 hours. Cover with plastic wrap and refrigerate for at least 6 hours before serving.

German Chocolate

CHEESECAKE

SERVES 10 TO 12

TIP
You can prepare the coconut mixture up to 3 days prior to use. Stir well before using.

VARIATION
Toasted almonds are a tasty substitute for pecans.

Preheat oven to 350°F (180°C)
9-inch (23 cm) cheesecake pan, ungreased, or springform pan with 3-inch (7.5 cm) sides, greased (for other pan sizes, see page 10)

CRUST

1¼ cups	chocolate sandwich cookie crumbs	300 mL
¼ cup	pecans, coarsely ground	50 mL
3 tbsp	unsalted butter, melted	45 mL

FILLING

1 cup	packed brown sugar	250 mL
2 tbsp	unsalted butter, softened	25 mL
2	egg yolks, stirred	2
1½ cups	flaked coconut	375 mL
¾ cup	pecan halves	175 mL
3	packages (each 8 oz/250 g) cream cheese, softened	3
1 cup	granulated sugar	250 mL
3	eggs	3
1 tsp	vanilla	5 mL
6 oz	bittersweet chocolate, melted and cooled	175 g

1. CRUST: In a medium bowl, combine cookie crumbs, pecans and butter. Press into bottom of cheesecake pan and freeze.

2. FILLING: In a medium saucepan on medium-high heat, melt brown sugar and butter for 3 minutes. Remove from heat. Slowly drizzle stirred egg yolks into mixture. Return to medium heat and stir for about 3 minutes. Add coconut and pecan halves. Cool for 20 minutes in the refrigerator. In a large mixer bowl, beat cream cheese and sugar on medium-high speed for 3 minutes. Add eggs, one at a time, beating after each addition. Stir in vanilla and melted chocolate. Fold half of the coconut mixture into batter. Set remainder aside for decorating. Pour batter over frozen crust. Bake in preheated oven for 45 to 55 minutes or until the top is light brown and the center has a slight jiggle to it. Cool on a rack for 2 hours. Cover with plastic wrap and refrigerate for at least 6 hours before decorating or serving.

3. DECORATION: Spread remaining coconut mixture on top of cake.

Milk Chocolate

CHEESECAKE ❦

SERVES 10 TO 12

TIP
Be careful not to blend the two cheesecake batters. If you do, swirl the chocolate into the vanilla and call it a Milk Chocolate Swirl Cheesecake.

VARIATION
Dust cocoa powder on top instead of shaved chocolate.

Preheat oven to 350°F (180°C)
9-inch (23 cm) cheesecake pan, ungreased, or springform pan with 3-inch (7.5 cm) sides, greased (for other pan sizes, see page 10)

CRUST

1½ cups	chocolate sandwich cookie crumbs	375 mL
¼ cup	unsalted butter, melted	50 mL

FILLING

4	packages (each 8 oz/250 g) cream cheese, softened	4
1¼ cups	granulated sugar	300 mL
4	eggs	4
1 cup	sour cream	250 mL
1 tbsp	vanilla	15 mL
4 oz	milk chocolate, melted and cooled	125 g

DECORATION

	Classic Whipped Cream Topping (see recipe, page 172)	
¼ cup	shaved chocolate	50 mL

1. CRUST: In a medium bowl, combine cookie crumbs and butter. Press into bottom of cheesecake pan and freeze.

2. FILLING: In a large mixer bowl, beat cream cheese and sugar on medium-high speed for 3 minutes. Add eggs, one at a time, beating after each addition. Mix in sour cream and vanilla. Divide mixture in half. Stir in cooled milk chocolate into one portion and pour over frozen crust. Pour remaining batter evenly over chocolate portion. Bake in preheated oven for 55 to 65 minutes or until the top is light brown and the center has a slight jiggle to it. Cool on a rack for 2 hours. Cover with plastic wrap and refrigerate for at least 6 hours before decorating or serving.

3. DECORATION: Ice top of cake with Classic Whipped Cream Topping or pipe rosettes around top of cake, if desired. Top with chocolate shavings.

Rocky Road

CHEESECAKE

Preheat oven to 350°F (180°C)
9-inch (23 cm) cheesecake pan, ungreased, or springform pan
with 3-inch (7.5 cm) sides, greased (for other pan sizes, see page 10)

> **M**y grandmother always had Rocky Road ice cream on hand for us because it was everybody's favorite. Here I've recreated that memorable taste in a cheesecake.

SERVES 10 TO 12

TIP
To melt chocolate in the microwave, break into squares and place in a microwave-safe dish. Microwave on high power for 1 to 2 minutes, stirring the mixture after 30 seconds.

VARIATION
Save a little time by substituting white chocolate chips for the decorative marshmallows and chocolate.

CRUST

1½ cups	chocolate sandwich cookie crumbs	375 mL
¼ cup	unsalted butter, melted	50 mL

FILLING

4	packages (each 8 oz/250 g) cream cheese, softened	4
1¼ cups	granulated sugar	300 mL
4	eggs	4
1 cup	sour cream	250 mL
1 tbsp	vanilla	15 mL
4 oz	bittersweet chocolate, melted and cooled	125 g
1 cup	walnuts, chopped and toasted	250 mL
1 cup	quartered large marshmallows	250 mL

DECORATION

½ cup	whipping (35%) cream	125 mL
2 tbsp	granulated sugar	25 mL
¼ cup	walnuts, chopped and toasted	50 mL
¼ cup	quartered large marshmallows	50 mL
2 oz	bittersweet chocolate, melted and cooled	60 g

1. CRUST: In a medium bowl, combine cookie crumbs and butter. Press into bottom of cheesecake pan and freeze.

2. FILLING: In a large bowl, beat cream cheese and sugar on medium-high for 3 minutes. Add eggs, one at a time, beating after each addition. Mix in sour cream and vanilla. Stir in melted chocolate. Fold in walnuts and marshmallows. Pour over frozen crust. Bake for 55 to 65 minutes or until the top is light brown. Cool for 2 hours. Cover and refrigerate for 6 hours before decorating.

3. DECORATION: In a well-chilled bowl, whip cream on medium-high speed until soft peaks form. With the mixer still running, sprinkle sugar into cream and continue whipping until firm peaks form. Pipe a border around edge of cake, if desired. Top with walnut and marshmallow pieces. Drizzle melted chocolate over top with a fork.

Triple-Chocolate

CHEESECAKE

Not two, but three chocolates make this a chocoholic's dream!

SERVES 10 TO 12

TIP
A small whisk is perfect for the small, but important, job of dissolving cocoa powder in hot water.

VARIATION
Dust additional cocoa powder on top and around the edge of the individual serving plates.

Preheat oven to 350°F (180°C)
9-inch (23 cm) cheesecake pan, ungreased, or springform pan
with 3-inch (7.5 cm) sides, greased (for other pan sizes, see page 10)

CRUST

1¼ cups	pecans, coarsely ground	300 mL
3 tbsp	all-purpose flour	45 mL
3 tbsp	unsalted butter, melted	45 mL

FILLING

¼ cup	unsweetened cocoa powder	50 mL
3 tbsp	hot water	45 mL
4	packages (each 8 oz/250 g) cream cheese, softened	4
1½ cups	granulated sugar	375 mL
5	eggs	5
2 tbsp	fresh lemon juice	25 mL
1 tsp	vanilla	5 mL
8 oz	bittersweet chocolate chunks	250 g
6 oz	white chocolate chunks	175 g

DECORATION

Fresh Raspberry Sauce
(see recipe, page 174)

1. CRUST: In a medium bowl, combine pecans, flour and butter. Press into bottom of cheesecake pan. Bake in preheated oven for 12 minutes. Cool until filling is ready.

2. FILLING: In a small bowl, dissolve cocoa powder in hot water. Set aside. In a large mixer bowl, beat cream cheese and sugar on medium-high speed for 3 minutes. Add eggs, one at a time, beating after each addition. Mix in lemon juice and vanilla. With a rubber spatula, fold in dissolved cocoa and chocolate chunks. Pour batter into baked crust. Bake in preheated oven for 45 to 55 minutes or until the top is light brown and the center has a slight jiggle to it. Cool on a rack for 2 hours. Cover with plastic wrap and refrigerate for at least 6 hours before decorating or serving.

3. DECORATION: Top each slice with a spoonful of Fresh Raspberry Sauce.

White Chocolate Raspberry

CHEESECAKE

This cheesecake reminds me of the pure white mountain caps of British Columbia. It will leave you with a cool feeling, too.

SERVES 10 TO 12

Preheat the oven to 400°F (200°C)
9-inch (23 cm) cheesecake or springform pan with 3-inch (7.5 cm) sides, sprayed with nonstick spray and bottom lined with parchment paper (for other pan sizes, see page 10)
13-by 9-inch (3 L) baking pan, filled with
2-inches (5 cm) boiling water

FILLING

3	packages (each 8 oz/250 g) cream cheese, softened	3
½ cup	granulated sugar	125 mL
1 tsp	fresh lemon juice	5 mL
½ tsp	salt	2 mL
12 oz	white chocolate, chopped and melted (see Tip, right)	375 g
1½ cups	sour cream	375 mL
4	eggs	4
1 tbsp	vanilla	15 mL
2½ cups	fresh raspberries	625 mL
1 tbsp	all-purpose flour	15 mL

TOPPING

1¾ cups	sour cream	425 mL
2 tbsp	granulated sugar	25 mL
½ tsp	vanilla	2 mL

DECORATION

	Fresh Raspberry Sauce (see recipe, page 174)	

1. FILLING: In a food processor, fitted with a metal blade, and in two batches, if necessary, combine cream cheese, sugar, lemon juice and salt for 30 seconds, scraping down sides of bowl. Add melted chocolate, sour cream, eggs and vanilla. Process for 30 seconds, scraping sides of bowl again. Process for one more minute. In a small bowl, toss berries with flour. With a rubber spatula, fold into chocolate mixture. Pour batter into bottom of prepared cheesecake pan.

2. Center cheesecake pan on the middle rack in the oven with a roasting pan of boiling water on the lower rack. Bake the cheesecake at 400°F (200°C) for 10 minutes. Reduce oven temperature to 350°F (180°C) and continue baking for about 45 to 55 minutes more or until top of cake is firm to the touch. Remove cheesecake from oven and place on a wire rack to cool for 10 minutes (do not turn the oven off).

2. TOPPING: In a small bowl, mix sour cream, sugar and vanilla. Pour into center of cooled cake and spread out to edges. Bake for 5 minutes more. Cool on a rack for 2 hours. Cover and refrigerate for at least 6 hours before decorating.

3. DECORATION: Garnish each individual serving slice with Fresh Raspberry Sauce.

Chocolate Macadamia

CHEESECAKE

Rich chocolate with rich Hawaiian macadamia nuts are a perfect marriage.

SERVES 10 TO 12

TIP
Cool the chocolate to room temperature before using to prevent it turning to chocolate chunks in the batter.

VARIATION
Pecans are a less expensive alternative to macadamia nuts.

Preheat oven to 350°F (180°C)
9-inch (23 cm) cheesecake pan, ungreased, or springform pan
with 3-inch (7.5 cm) sides, greased (for other pan sizes, see page 10)

CRUST

1 1/4 cups	chocolate sandwich cookies crumbs	300 mL
3 tbsp	unsalted butter, melted	45 mL

FILLING

3	packages (each 8 oz/250 g) cream cheese, softened	3
1 cup	granulated sugar	250 mL
3	eggs	3
2	egg yolks	2
1 tsp	vanilla	5 mL
6 oz	bittersweet chocolate, melted and cooled	175 g
1 cup	macadamia nuts, chopped and toasted	250 mL

DECORATION

	Classic Whipped Cream Topping (see recipe, page 172)	
1/4 cup	macadamia nuts, chopped and toasted	50 mL

1. CRUST: In a medium bowl, combine cookie crumbs and butter. Press into bottom of cheesecake pan and freeze.

2. FILLING: In a large mixer bowl, beat cream cheese and sugar on medium-high speed for 3 minutes. Add eggs and egg yolks, one at a time, beating after each addition. Add vanilla and melted chocolate. Fold in macadamia nuts. Pour batter over frozen crust. Bake in preheated oven for 45 to 55 minutes or until the top is light brown and the center has a slight jiggle to it. Cool on a rack for 2 hours. Cover with plastic wrap and refrigerate for at least 6 hours before decorating or serving.

3. DECORATING: Ice top of cake with Classic Whipped Cream Topping or pipe a border around the edge of cake, if desired. Sprinkle with toasted macadamia nuts.

Citrus Cheesecakes

Blood Orange

CHEESECAKE

B*lood oranges are available in early spring. The outside skin is orange with red splotches. The fruit and juice are a deep red-orange color and very sweet.*

SERVES 10 TO 12

TIPS

Substitute a navel orange instead of the blood orange. The cheesecake will not be as sweet.

If you find blood oranges, purchase a box and zest them one day and then juice them the next. The juice and zest can be frozen for up to 6 months.

Preheat oven to 350°F (180°C)
9-inch (23 cm) cheesecake pan, ungreased, or springform pan with 3-inch (7.5 cm) sides, greased (for other pan sizes, see page 10)

CRUST

1 1/4 cups	butter cookie crumbs	300 mL
1/4 cup	pecans, toasted and ground	50 mL
3 tbsp	unsalted butter, melted	45 mL

FILLING

3	packages (each 8 oz/250 g) cream cheese, softened	3
1/2 cup	sour cream	125 mL
1 1/2 cups	small curd cottage cheese, drained (see Tip, page 36)	375 mL
1 1/2 cups	granulated sugar	375 mL
4	eggs	4
1/4 cup	all-purpose flour	50 mL
1 tbsp	blood orange zest	15 mL
1/3 cup	blood orange juice	75 mL
1 tsp	ground nutmeg	5 mL
1 tsp	vanilla	5 mL

TOPPING

1/2 cup	sour cream	125 mL
1/4 cup	granulated sugar	50 mL
1 tbsp	blood orange zest	15 mL
2 tbsp	blood orange juice	25 mL
1/2 tsp	vanilla	2 mL

DECORATION

1/2 cup	heavy cream	125 mL
2 tbsp	granulated sugar	25 mL
1/4 tsp	blood orange zest	1 mL

1. CRUST: In a medium bowl, combine cookie crumbs, pecans and butter. Press into bottom of cheesecake pan and freeze.

2. FILLING: In a large mixer bowl, beat cream cheese, sour cream, cottage cheese and sugar on medium-high speed for 3 minutes. Add eggs, one at a time, beating after each addition. Mix in flour, blood orange juice, zest, nutmeg and vanilla. Pour over frozen crust. Bake in preheated oven for 45 to 55 minutes or until the top is light brown and the center has a slight jiggle to it. Cool on the counter for 10 minutes (do not turn the oven off). The cake will sink slightly.

3. TOPPING: In a small bowl, combine sour cream, sugar, blood orange zest, juice and vanilla. Pour mixture into center of cooled cake and spread out to edges. Bake for 5 minutes more. Cool on a rack for 2 hours. Cover and refrigerate for at least 6 hours before decorating or serving.

4. DECORATION: In a well-chilled bowl, whip cream on medium-high speed until soft peaks form. With the mixer still running, sprinkle sugar into cream and continue whipping until firm peaks form. Ice top of cake with whipped cream or pipe rosettes around top of cake, if desired. Sprinkle with zest.

Mandarin Orange

CHESECAKE

Preheat oven to 350°F (180°C)

*9-inch (23 cm) cheesecake pan, ungreased, or springform pan
with 3-inch (7.5 cm) sides, greased (for other pan sizes, see page 10)*

> T his cheesecake is
> a great dessert after
> spicy Asian food.

SERVES 10 TO 12

TIP
Fresh mandarin
oranges are usually
available in
November and
December for the
peak holiday baking
season. Store in the
refrigerator as they
spoil quickly,
and wash well
before zesting.

CRUST

1 cup	graham cracker crumbs	250 mL
¾ cup	almonds, toasted and coarsely ground	175 mL
¼ cup	unsalted butter, melted	50 mL

FILLING

3	packages (each 8 oz/250 g) cream cheese, softened	3
½ cup	unsalted butter, softened	125 mL
1 cup	granulated sugar	250 mL
4	eggs	4
½ cup	sour cream	125 mL
1½ tbsp	orange zest	22 mL
¼ cup	orange juice concentrate	50 mL
1 tsp	vanilla	5 mL
1	can (10 oz/300 mL) mandarin orange segments, drained	1

TOPPING

1½ cups	sour cream	375 mL
2 tbsp	granulated sugar	25 mL
2 tbsp	fresh orange juice	25 mL

DECORATION

½ cup	whipping cream	125 mL
2 tbsp	granulated sugar	25 mL

VARIATION
You can substitute
clementines for the
mandarin oranges.

1. CRUST: In a medium bowl, combine graham cracker crumbs, almonds and butter. Press into bottom of cheesecake pan and freeze.

2. FILLING: In a large mixer bowl, beat cream cheese, butter and sugar on medium-high speed for 3 minutes. Add eggs, one at a time, beating after each addition. Mix in sour cream, orange zest, orange juice concentrate and vanilla. Fold orange segments into batter. Pour batter into frozen crust. Bake in preheated oven for 45 to 55 minutes or until the top is light brown and the center has a slight jiggle to it. Cool on the counter for 10 minutes (do not turn the oven off). The cake will sink slightly.

3. TOPPING: In a small bowl, combine sour cream, sugar, and orange juice. Pour mixture into center of cooled cake and spread out to edges. Bake for 5 minutes more. Cool on a rack for 2 hours. Cover and refrigerate for at least 6 hours before decorating or serving.

4. DECORATION: In a well-chilled bowl, whip cream on medium-high speed until soft peaks form. With the mixer still running, sprinkle sugar into cream and continue whipping until firm peaks form. Ice top of cake or pipe a border around cake, if desired.

Orange Honey Ricotta
CHEESECAKE

Preheat oven to 300°F (150°C)
9-inch (23 cm) cheesecake pan, ungreased, or springform pan
with 3-inch (7.5 cm) sides, greased (for other pan sizes, see page 10)

CRUST

1 1/4 cups	graham cracker crumbs	300 mL
1 tbsp	unsalted butter, melted	15 mL
2 tsp	liquid honey	10 mL

FILLING

4 oz	cream cheese, softened	125 g
1/2 cup	liquid honey	125 mL
2 cups	ricotta cheese, drained (see Tip, page 25)	500 mL
1/2 cup	plain yogurt	125 mL
1 tsp	cornstarch	5 ml
2	eggs	2
2 tsp	orange zest	10 mL
1 tbsp	orange juice concentrate	15 mL
1/4 tsp	salt	1 mL
3	egg whites	3

DECORATION

2	medium oranges	2
2 tbsp	liquid honey	25 mL

1. CRUST: In a medium bowl, combine graham cracker crumbs, butter and honey. Press into bottom of cheesecake pan and freeze.

2. FILLING: In a large mixer bowl, beat cream cheese, honey and ricotta cheese on medium-high speed for 3 minutes. Add eggs, one at a time, beating after each addition. Beat in yogurt, cornstarch, orange zest, orange juice concentrate and salt. Set aside. In a clean mixing bowl, whip egg whites on medium-high speed until firm peaks form. Carefully fold into cheese batter. Pour batter over frozen crust. Bake in preheated oven for 50 to 60 minutes or until the top is light brown and the center has a slight jiggle to it. Cool on a rack for 2 hours. Cover with plastic wrap and refrigerate for at least 6 hours before decorating or serving.

3. DECORATION: Remove white pith and peel from oranges and cut into very thin slices. Arrange slices on top of cake. In a small saucepan on low, heat honey. Using a pastry brush, brush hot honey over orange slices. Chill before serving.

Lemon Curd Swirl
CHEESECAKE

Preheat oven to 325°F (160°C)
9-inch (23 cm) cheesecake pan, ungreased, or springform pan with 3-inch (7.5 cm) sides, greased (for other pan sizes, see page 10)

CRUST

1½ cups	lemon cookie crumbs	375 mL
¼ cup	unsalted butter, melted	50 mL

FILLING

5	egg yolks	5
⅓ cup	granulated sugar	75 mL
¼ cup	fresh lemon juice	50 mL
¼ cup	unsalted butter, softened	50 mL
3	packages (each 8 oz/250 g) cream cheese, softened	3
¾ cup	granulated sugar	175 mL
3	eggs	3
2 tbsp	lemon zest	25 mL
1 tbsp	fresh lemon juice	15 mL
1 tsp	vanilla	5 mL

DECORATION

Classic Whipped Cream Topping
(see recipe, page 172)

1. CRUST: In a medium bowl, combine cookie crumbs and butter. Press into bottom of cheesecake pan and freeze.

2. FILLING: Bring water to a simmer in the bottom of a double boiler. In the top of double boiler, away from heat, whisk yolks. Sprinkle sugar in while whisking. Pour in lemon juice in a steady stream while whisking. Place top part of double boiler over the simmering water. Cook, stirring constantly, until thick, about 7 minutes. Whisk in butter. Set aside to cool in a bowl. In a large bowl, beat cream cheese and sugar on medium-high for 3 minutes. Add eggs, one at a time, beating after each addition. Mix in zest, juice and vanilla. Reserve half of cooled lemon mixture for the topping. Swirl remaining half into batter. Pour over crust. Bake for 45 to 55 minutes or until the top is light brown. Cool for 2 hours. Cover and refrigerate for 6 hours before decorating.

3. DECORATING: Spread remaining lemon mixture in the center, about 1½ inches (4 cm) from the edge. Pipe a whipped cream border around top of cake.

Meyer Lemon

CHEESECAKE

Preheat oven to 325°F (160°C)
9-inch (23 cm) cheesecake pan, ungreased, or springform pan
with 3-inch (7.5 cm) sides, greased (for other pan sizes, see page 10)

Meyer lemons are found in southern California and the south of France. A cross between a lemon and a mandarin, Meyers have a slight floral essence and delicate lemon flavor.

SERVES 10 TO 12

TIPS
If you can't find Meyer lemons, mix equal parts orange and lemon juice to try to approximate their sweet fragrance and flavor.

Treat yourself to a box of Meyer lemons and make juice to keep handy in the freezer.

VARIATION
Top cake with fresh blueberries.

CRUST

1½ cups	lemon cookie crumbs	375 mL
¼ cup	unsalted butter, melted	50 mL

FILLING

2	packages (each 8 oz/250 g) cream cheese, softened	2
¾ cup	granulated sugar	175 mL
3	eggs	3
2 tbsp	Meyer lemon zest	25 mL
2 tbsp	fresh Meyer lemon juice (see Tip, left)	25 mL
1 tsp	vanilla	5 mL

TOPPING

½ cup	sour cream	125 mL
¼ cup	granulated sugar	50 mL
1 tbsp	fresh Meyer lemon juice	15 mL
½ tsp	vanilla	2 mL

1. CRUST: In a medium bowl, combine cookie crumbs and butter. Press into bottom of cheesecake pan and freeze.

2. FILLING: In a large mixer bowl, beat cream cheese and sugar on medium-high speed for 3 minutes. Add eggs, one at a time, beating after each addition. Mix in zest, juice and vanilla. Pour over frozen crust. Bake in preheated oven for 45 to 55 minutes or until the top is light brown and the center has a slight jiggle to it. Cool on the counter for 10 minutes (do not turn the oven off). The cake will sink slightly.

3. TOPPING: In a small bowl, combine sour cream, sugar, lemon juice and vanilla. Pour mixture into center of cooled cake and spread out to edges. Bake for 5 minutes more. Cool on a rack for 2 hours. Cover and refrigerate for at least 6 hours before serving.

Lemon Meringue

CHEESECAKE

Before preheating oven, position lowest oven rack as far away from heat source as possible.
Preheat oven to 350°F (180°C)
9-inch (23 cm) cheesecake pan, ungreased, or springform pan with 3-inch (7.5 cm) sides, greased (for other pan sizes, see page 10)

M y sister Monica never wanted a cake for her birthday. She always asked for Lemon Meringue Pie, which inspired this recipe. It's just like a pie, but it's a cheesecake!

SERVES 10 TO 12

TIPS

Room temperature egg whites yield a much higher volume than cold whites.

Use a kitchen torch to brown the meringue instead of the oven.

CRUST

1	package (6 oz/175 g) flaked coconut, toasted to light brown (see Tip, page 59)	1
¼ cup	chopped pecans, toasted	50 mL
3 tbsp	unsalted butter, melted	45 mL

FILLING

2	packages (each 8 oz/250 g) cream cheese, softened	2
⅓ cup	granulated sugar	75 mL
3	egg yolks	3
¼ cup	fresh lemon juice	50 mL
1 tsp	vanilla	5 mL

TOPPING

3	egg whites	3
Dash	salt	Dash
1	jar (7.5 oz/210 g) marshmallow cream (fluff)	1
½ cup	chopped pecans, toasted	125 mL

1. CRUST: In a medium bowl, combine coconut, pecans and butter. Press into bottom of cheesecake pan and freeze.

2. FILLING: In a large mixer bowl, beat cream cheese and sugar on medium-high speed for 3 minutes. Add eggs yolks, one at a time, beating after each addition. Mix in lemon juice and vanilla. Pour over frozen crust. Bake for 40 to 50 minutes or until light brown and the center has a slight jiggle to it. Set on a wire rack to cool while you prepare the topping. Turn the oven to broil.

3. TOPPING: In a clean mixing bowl, whip egg whites and salt until foamy. Gradually add marshmallow cream, beating until stiff peaks form. Sprinkle top of cake with chopped pecans. Spread the marshmallow mixture on top of pecans. Place in oven on lowest oven rack and broil until the top meringue is light brown.

Lemon Soufflé

CHEESECAKE

Preheat oven to 325°F (160°C)
9-inch (23 cm) cheesecake pan, ungreased, or springform pan
with 3-inch (7.5 cm) sides, greased (for other pan sizes, see page 10)

W*hile dining
in Los Angeles
at Ciudad, I had
a wonderful
cheesecake that was
so light and airy, I
had to create my
own version in
homage to Chefs
Milliken and Feniger.*

SERVES 10 TO 12

TIP
Save extra egg yolks
in the refrigerator for
up to 2 days in a
small bowl by cover-
ing in water and seal-
ing tightly with
plastic wrap. To
freeze, sprinkle salt or
sugar over the yolks
in water.

CRUST

1½ cups	butter cookie crumbs	375 mL
¼ cup	unsalted butter, melted	50 mL

FILLING

4	packages (each 8 oz/250 g) cream cheese, softened	4
½ cup	sour cream	125 mL
1½ cups	granulated sugar	375 mL
4	egg yolks	4
1 tbsp	lemon zest	15 mL
3 tbsp	fresh lemon juice	45 mL
1½ tsp	vanilla	7 mL
6	egg whites	6
¼ tsp	cream of tartar	1 mL

DECORATION

¼ cup	confectioner's (icing) sugar	50 mL

1. CRUST: In a medium bowl, combine cookie crumbs and butter. Press into bottom of cheesecake pan and freeze.

2. FILLING: In a large mixer bowl, beat cream cheese, sour cream and sugar on medium-high speed for 3 minutes. Add eggs yolks, one at a time, beating after each addition. Beat in zest, juice and vanilla. Set aside. In a clean mixing bowl with whip attachment, whip egg whites and cream of tartar on low speed for 1 minute. Increase speed to medium high and whip until stiff peaks form, but not dry. Fold into cream cheese mixture carefully so as not to deflate the mixture. Pour batter over frozen crust. Bake in preheated oven for 40 to 45 minutes or until the top is light brown and the center has a slight jiggle to it. Cool on a rack for 2 hours. Cover with plastic wrap and refrigerate for at least 6 hours before decorating or serving.

3. DECORATION: Dust top of chilled cake with a sprinkling of confectioner's sugar using a sugar dredger or flour sifter.

South of France Lemon

CHEESECAKE

SERVES 10 TO 12

TIPS

It is very important to drain the ricotta overnight. Otherwise you will have too much liquid.

This cheesecake is quite a different texture than the others in this book. Don't look for doneness by browning or a jiggley center.

Make a dessert cheese course by serving fresh fruit on the side.

Preheat oven to 300°F (150°C)
9-inch (23 cm) cheesecake or springform pan with 3-inch (7.5 cm) sides, lined with parchment paper (for other pan sizes, see page 10)

2 lbs	ricotta cheese, drained overnight (see Tip, page 25)	1 kg
⅔ cup	granulated sugar	150 mL
⅓ cup	all-purpose flour	75 mL
6	eggs	6
2 tsp	orange zest	10 mL
2 tsp	lemon zest	10 mL
1 tbsp	lemon juice	15 mL
¼ tsp	ground cinnamon	1 mL
2 tsp	vanilla	10 mL

1. In a large bowl, stir ricotta cheese with a rubber spatula until creamy. Add sugar and flour, mixing until blended. Add eggs, one at a time, stirring after each addition. Stir in orange and lemon zests, juice, cinnamon and vanilla. Pour into prepared cheesecake pan. Bake for 75 to 90 minutes or until tip of knife inserted in the center comes out clean. Cool on rack for 2 hours. Cover and refrigerate for at least 6 hours before serving.

Florida Key Lime

CHEESECAKE

SERVES 10 TO 12

TIP
If Key limes are unavailable, substitute half Persian lime juice and half lemon juice
for the amount of juice called for in the recipe.

VARIATION
A thin twisted slice of lime makes an easy pretty garnish for a last-minute touch.

Preheat oven to 325°F (160°C)
9-inch (23 cm) cheesecake pan, ungreased, or springform pan with 3-inch (7.5 cm) sides, greased (for other pan sizes, see page 10)

CRUST

1½ cups	butter cookies crumbs	375 mL
¼ cup	unsalted butter, melted	50 mL

FILLING

4	packages (each 8 oz/250 g) cream cheese, softened	4
1½ cups	granulated sugar	375 mL
2	eggs	2
2	egg yolks	2
1 tbsp	Key lime zest (see Tip, left)	15 mL
¼ cup	fresh Key lime juice	50 mL
1 tsp	vanilla	5 mL

TOPPING

½ cup	sour cream	125 mL
¼ cup	granulated sugar	50 mL
1 tsp	Key lime zest	5 mL
1 tbsp	fresh Key lime juice	15 mL
½ tsp	vanilla	2 mL

1. CRUST: In a medium bowl, combine cookie crumbs and butter. Press into bottom of cheesecake pan and freeze.

2. FILLING: In a large mixer bowl, beat cream cheese and sugar on medium-high speed for 3 minutes. Add eggs and egg yolks, one at a time, beating after each addition. Mix in lime zest, juice and vanilla. Pour over frozen crust. Bake for 45 to 55 minutes or until the top is light brown. Cool for 10 minutes (do not turn the oven off). The cake will sink slightly.

3. TOPPING: In a bowl, combine sour cream, sugar, lime zest, juice and vanilla. Pour into center of cooled cake and spread to edges. Bake for 5 minutes more. Cool for 2 hours. Cover and refrigerate for 6 hours before serving.

Lime Curd

CHEESECAKE 🦋

Preheat oven to 325°F (160°C)
9-inch (23 cm) cheesecake pan, ungreased, or springform pan
with 3-inch (7.5 cm) sides, greased (for other pan sizes, see page 10)

T*he tart lime paired with the sweet filling creates a refreshing taste for a spring dessert.*

🦋

SERVES 10 TO 12

TIP
Extra egg whites can be stored in the refrigerator for up to 4 days or frozen for up to 6 months.

CRUST

1 1/2 cups	butter cookie crumbs	375 mL
1/4 cup	unsalted butter, melted	50 mL

FILLING

5	egg yolks	5
1/3 cup	granulated sugar	75 mL
1/4 cup	fresh lime juice	50 mL
1/4 cup	unsalted butter, softened	50 mL
3	packages (each 8 oz/250 g) cream cheese, softened	3
3/4 cup	granulated sugar	175 mL
3	eggs	3
2 tbsp	lime zest	25 mL
1 tbsp	fresh lime juice	15 mL
1 tsp	vanilla	5 mL

DECORATION

Classic Whipped Cream Topping
(see recipe, page 172)

1. CRUST: In a medium bowl, combine cookie crumbs and butter. Press into bottom of cheesecake pan and freeze.

2. FILLING: Bring water to a simmer in the bottom of a double boiler. In the top of double boiler, away from heat, whisk yolks. Sprinkle sugar in while whisking. Pour in lime juice in a steady stream while whisking. Place top part of double boiler over the simmering water. Cook, stirring constantly, until thick, about 7 minutes. Whisk in butter. Set aside to cool in a bowl. In a large bowl, beat cream cheese and sugar on medium-high speed for 3 minutes. Add eggs, one at a time, beating after each addition. Mix in zest, juice and vanilla. Reserve half of the cooled lime mixture for the topping. Swirl remaining half into batter. Pour over crust. Bake for 45 to 55 minutes or until the top is light brown. Cool for 2 hours. Cover and refrigerate for 6 hours before decorating or serving.

3. DECORATION: Spread remaining lime mixture in the center, about 1 1/2 inches (4 cm) from the edge of the cake. Pipe a whipped cream border around top of cake.

Lime Soufflé
CHEESECAKE ❦

Preheat oven to 325°F (160°C)
9-inch (23 cm) cheesecake pan, ungreased, or springform pan with 3-inch (7.5 cm) sides, greased (for other pan sizes, see page 10)

CRUST

1½ cups	butter cookie crumbs	375 mL
¼ cup	unsalted butter, melted	50 mL

FILLING

4	packages (each 8 oz/250 g) cream cheese, softened	4
½ cup	sour cream	125 mL
1½ cups	granulated sugar	375 mL
4	egg yolks	4
1 tbsp	lime zest	15 mL
2 tbsp	fresh lime juice	25 mL
1½ tsp	vanilla	7 mL
6	egg whites (see Tip, page 89)	6
¼ tsp	cream of tartar	1 mL

DECORATION

¼ cup	confectioner's (icing) sugar	50 mL

1. CRUST: In a medium bowl, combine cookie crumbs and butter. Press into bottom of cheesecake pan and freeze.

2. FILLING: In a large mixer bowl, beat cream cheese, sour cream and sugar on medium-high speed for 3 minutes. Add egg yolks, one at a time, beating after each addition. Beat in zest, juice and vanilla. Set aside. In a clean mixing bowl with whip attachment, whip egg whites and cream of tartar on low speed for 1 minute. Increase speed to medium high and whip until stiff peaks form, but not dry. Fold into cream cheese mixture carefully so as not to deflate the mixture. Pour batter over frozen crust. Bake in preheated oven for 45 to 55 minutes or until the top is light brown and the center has a slight jiggle to it. Cool on a rack for 2 hours. Cover with plastic wrap and refrigerate for at least 6 hours before decorating or serving.

3. DECORATION: Dust top of chilled cake with a sprinkling of confectioner's sugar using a sugar dredger or flour sifter.

No-Bake Cheesecakes

Berry Berry Berry

CHEESECAKE ❧

This cheesecake bursts with the flavor of three different kinds of berries folded into the batter. ❧

SERVES 10 TO 12

TIP
Wash and dry berries completely before using.

VARIATION
If you must substitute frozen berries, fold them in while still frozen.

9-inch (23 cm) cheesecake pan, ungreased, or springform pan with 3-inch (7.5 cm) sides, greased (for other pan sizes, see page 10)

CRUST

1½ cups	butter cookie crumbs	375 mL
3 tbsp	unsalted butter, melted	45 mL

FILLING

1	packet (¼ oz/7.5 g) powdered unflavored gelatin	1
¼ cup	milk	50 mL
2	packages (each 8 oz/250 g) cream cheese, softened	2
1 cup	granulated sugar	250 mL
1 tbsp	fresh lemon juice	15 mL
2 tsp	vanilla	10 mL
1 cup	whipping (35%) cream, whipped	250 mL
1 cup	fresh strawberries, crushed	250 mL
1 cup	fresh blackberries, crushed	250 mL
1 cup	fresh raspberries, crushed	250 mL

DECORATION

	Classic Whipped Cream Topping (see recipe, page 172)	
1 cup	mixed berries, such as strawberries, blackberries and raspberries	250 mL

1. CRUST: In a medium bowl, combine butter cookie crumbs and butter. Press into bottom of cheesecake pan and freeze.

2. FILLING: Sprinkle gelatin over milk in a small saucepan and let stand for 1 minute. Stir over low heat until gelatin is completely dissolved. Set aside to cool slightly. In a mixer bowl, beat cream cheese and sugar on medium speed for 3 minutes. Slowly add dissolved gelatin. Mix in lemon juice and vanilla. Fold in whipped cream. Fold in berries. Pour over frozen crust. Chill until firm, about 6 hours. Run a hot knife around edge of pan to loosen.

3. DECORATION: Ice top of cake with Classic Whipped Cream Topping or pipe rosettes around top of cake, if desired. Garnish with berries.

Mandarin Orange Cheesecake (page 84) ➤
Overleaf: Chocolate Peanut Butter Cheese Bars (page 124)

Raspberry Cream

CHEESECAKE

You don't have to heat up the oven for this no-bake perfect treat. Enjoy it with friends during a hot summer day.

SERVES 10 TO 12

TIP
It's easier to get the marshmallow cream out of the jar with a hot spatula. Run hot water over the spatula to warm it.

VARIATION
Try strawberries or blueberries in place of the raspberries.

9-inch (23 cm) cheesecake pan, ungreased, or springform pan with 3-inch (7.5 cm) sides, greased (for other pan sizes, see page 10)

CRUST

1½ cups	butter cookie crumbs	375 mL
3 tbsp	unsalted butter, melted	45 mL

FILLING

1	packet (¼ oz/7.5 g) powdered unflavored gelatin	1
¼ cup	milk	50 mL
2	packages (each 8 oz/250 g) cream cheese, softened	2
1 tbsp	fresh lemon juice	15 mL
2 tsp	vanilla	10 mL
1	jar (7.5 oz/210 g) marshmallow cream (fluff)	1
1 cup	whipping (35%) cream	250 mL
¼ cup	granulated sugar	50 mL
2 cups	fresh raspberries, crushed	500 mL

DECORATION

	Classic Whipped Cream Topping (see recipe, page 172)	
1 cup	fresh raspberries, whole	250 mL

1. CRUST: In a medium bowl, combine cookie crumbs and butter. Press into bottom of cheesecake pan and freeze.

2. FILLING: Sprinkle gelatin over milk in a small saucepan and let stand for 1 minute. Stir over low heat until gelatin is completely dissolved. Set aside to cool slightly. In a mixer bowl, beat cream cheese on medium for 3 minutes. Slowly add dissolved gelatin. Mix in lemon juice and vanilla. Add marshmallow cream, beating on medium until blended. Set aside. In a well-chilled bowl, whip cream on medium-high until soft peaks form. With the mixer still running, sprinkle sugar into cream and continue whipping until firm peaks form. Fold whipped cream and crushed raspberries into the mixture. Pour over frozen crust. Chill until firm, about 6 hours. Run a hot knife around edge of pan to loosen.

3. DECORATION: Ice top of cake with Classic Whipped Cream Topping or pipe rosettes around top of cake, if desired. Garnish with raspberries.

◄ Lemon Soufflé Cheesecake (page 90)
Overleaf: Mini-Lemon Cheesecake (page 122)

Orange Citrus

CHEESECAKE

SERVES 10 TO 12

TIP
Orange juice does not have as much flavor as concentrate. If you have juice but not concentrate, reduce it by half over low heat to intensify the flavor.

VARIATION
Add 2 tbsp (25 mL) orange-flavored liqueur to further highlight the citrus flavor.

9-inch (23 cm) cheesecake pan, ungreased, or springform pan with 3-inch (7.5 cm) sides, greased (for other pan sizes, see page 10)

CRUST

1 1/4 cups	butter cookie crumbs	300 mL
3 tbsp	unsalted butter, melted	45 mL

FILLING

1	packet (1/4 oz/7.5 g) powdered unflavored gelatin	1
1/2 cup	orange juice concentrate	125 mL
3	packages (each 8 oz/250 g) cream cheese, softened	3
3/4 cup	granulated sugar	175 mL
1 tsp	vanilla	5 mL
1/4 tsp	orange zest	1 mL
1 cup	whipping (35%) cream, whipped	250 mL

DECORATION

	Classic Whipped Cream Topping (see recipe, page 172)	
1/4 tsp	orange zest	1 mL

1. CRUST: In a medium bowl, combine cookie crumbs and butter. Press into bottom of cheesecake pan and freeze.

2. FILLING: Sprinkle gelatin over orange juice in a small saucepan and let stand for 1 minute. Stir over low heat until gelatin is completely dissolved. Set aside to cool slightly. In a mixer bowl, beat cream cheese and sugar on medium speed for 3 minutes. Slowly add dissolved gelatin. Add vanilla and orange zest, mixing until blended. Fold in whipped cream. Pour over frozen crust. Chill until firm, about 6 hours. Run a hot knife around edge of pan to loosen.

3. DECORATION: Ice top of cake with Classic Whipped Cream Topping or pipe rosettes around top of cake, if desired. Sprinkle orange zest on top.

Chocolate Mocha Chunk

CHEESECAKE

SERVES 10 TO 12

TIP
You can whip the cream up to 2 hours prior to making the cheesecake so it is ready when you need it. Keep in refrigerator until ready to use.

VARIATION
Add 2 tbsp (25 mL) coffee-flavored liqueur for an extra mocha punch when adding the vanilla.

9-inch (23 cm) cheesecake pan, ungreased, or springform pan with 3-inch (7.5 cm) sides, greased (for other pan sizes, see page 10)

CRUST

1 1/4 cups	chocolate cookie crumbs	300 mL
3 tbsp	unsalted butter, melted	45 mL

FILLING

2	packets (each 1/4 oz/7.5 g) powdered unflavored gelatin	2
1/2 cup	milk	125 mL
4	packages (each 8 oz/250 g) cream cheese, softened	4
1 1/2 cups	granulated sugar	375 mL
2/3 cup	unsweetened cocoa powder, sifted	150 mL
1/4 cup	instant coffee powder	50 mL
1 tbsp	hot water	15 mL
1 tsp	vanilla	5 mL
12 oz	bittersweet chocolate chunks	375 g
2 cups	whipping (35%) cream, whipped	500 mL

DECORATION

	Classic Whipped Cream Topping (see recipe, page 172)	
3 oz	bittersweet chocolate	90 g

1. **CRUST:** In a medium bowl, combine cookie crumbs and butter. Press into bottom of cheesecake pan and freeze.

2. **FILLING:** Sprinkle gelatin over milk in a small saucepan and let stand for 1 minute. Stir over low heat until gelatin is dissolved. Set aside to cool slightly. In a bowl, beat cream cheese and sugar on medium-high for 3 minutes. Slowly add dissolved gelatin. Stir in cocoa powder. In a small bowl, dissolve coffee powder and hot water. Stir into cream cheese mixture. Stir in vanilla and chocolate chunks. Fold in whipped cream. Pour over crust. Chill until firm, about 6 hours. Run a hot knife around edge of pan to loosen.

3. **DECORATION:** Ice top of cake with Classic Whipped Cream Topping, if desired. Grate chocolate over cake.

Cookies and Cream

CHEESECAKE

9-inch (23 cm) cheesecake pan, ungreased, or springform pan with 3-inch (7.5 cm) sides, greased (for other pan sizes, see page 10)

The cookies and cream combination started a sensation in ice cream, then cake, and now cheesecake.

SERVES 10 TO 12

TIP
Make sure your cream cheese is room temperature prior to making this cheesecake.

VARIATION
Any type of cookie works well in this recipe.

CRUST

1¼ cups	chocolate cookie crumbs	300 mL
3 tbsp	unsalted butter, melted	45 mL

FILLING

1	packet (¼ oz/7.5 g) powdered unflavored gelatin	1
¼ cup	milk	50 mL
2	packages (each 8 oz/250 g) cream cheese, softened	2
¾ cup	granulated sugar	175 mL
1½ tsp	vanilla	7 mL
2 cups	slightly crushed chocolate sandwich cookies, about 16	500 mL
1 cup	whipping (35%) cream, whipped	250 mL

DECORATION

	Classic Whipped Cream Topping (see recipe, page 172)	
12	chocolate sandwich cookies, crumbled	12

1. CRUST: In a medium bowl, combine cookie crumbs and butter. Press into bottom of cheesecake pan and freeze.

2. FILLING: Sprinkle gelatin over milk in a small saucepan and let stand for 1 minute. Stir over low heat until gelatin is completely dissolved. Set aside to cool slightly. In a mixer bowl, beat cream cheese and sugar on medium speed for 3 minutes. Slowly add dissolved gelatin. Stir in vanilla. Fold in crushed cookies and whipped cream. Pour over frozen crust. Chill until firm, about 6 hours. Run a hot knife around edge of pan to loosen.

3. DECORATION: Ice top of cake with Classic Whipped Cream Topping, if desired. Crumble cookies on top.

Holiday Rum Eggnog

CHESECAKE

9-inch (23 cm) cheesecake pan, ungreased, or springform pan with 3-inch (7.5 cm) sides, greased (for other pan sizes, see page 10)

(for other pan sizes, see page 10)

<table>
<tr><td colspan="3">CRUST</td></tr>
<tr><td>1 1/4 cups</td><td>gingersnap cookie crumbs</td><td>300 mL</td></tr>
<tr><td>3 tbsp</td><td>unsalted butter, melted</td><td>45 mL</td></tr>
<tr><td colspan="3">FILLING</td></tr>
<tr><td>2</td><td>packets (each 1/4 oz/7.5 g) powdered unflavored gelatin</td><td>2</td></tr>
<tr><td>1/4 cup</td><td>milk</td><td>50 mL</td></tr>
<tr><td>2</td><td>packages (each 8 oz/250 g) cream cheese, softened</td><td>2</td></tr>
<tr><td>1/4 cup</td><td>granulated sugar</td><td>50 mL</td></tr>
<tr><td>1 cup</td><td>prepared eggnog</td><td>250 mL</td></tr>
<tr><td>1/4 cup</td><td>light rum</td><td>50 mL</td></tr>
<tr><td>1 1/2 tsp</td><td>vanilla</td><td>7 mL</td></tr>
<tr><td>1/2 tsp</td><td>ground nutmeg</td><td>2 mL</td></tr>
<tr><td>1 cup</td><td>whipping (35%) cream, whipped</td><td>250 mL</td></tr>
<tr><td colspan="3">DECORATION</td></tr>
<tr><td></td><td>Classic Whipped Cream Topping (see recipe, page 172)</td><td></td></tr>
<tr><td>1/4 tsp</td><td>ground nutmeg</td><td>1 mL</td></tr>
</table>

H*ere's a perfect dessert to make when the turkey is taking up all of the room in the oven.*

SERVES 10 TO 12

TIP
If gingersnaps are difficult to find you can use graham crackers with 1 tsp (5 mL) ground ginger blended in.

VARIATION
Apple juice is a non-alcoholic substitute for rum.

1. CRUST: In a medium bowl, combine cookie crumbs and butter. Press into bottom of cheesecake pan and freeze.

2. FILLING: Sprinkle gelatin over milk in a small saucepan and let stand for 1 minute. Stir over low heat until gelatin is completely dissolved. Set aside to cool slightly. In a mixer bowl, beat cream cheese and sugar on medium speed for 3 minutes. Slowly add dissolved gelatin. Beat in eggnog, rum, vanilla and nutmeg. Fold in whipped cream. Pour over frozen crust, smoothing it out to touch sides of pan. Chill until firm, about 6 hours. Run a hot knife around edge of pan to loosen.

3. DECORATION: Ice top of cake with Classic Whipped Cream Topping, if desired. Dust with a sprinkling of nutmeg.

Irish Cream

CHEESECAKE ❧

9-inch (23 cm) cheesecake pan, ungreased, or springform pan with 3-inch (7.5 cm) sides, greased (for other pan sizes, see page 10)

<table>
<tr><td colspan="4">CRUST</td></tr>
</table>

1½ cups	graham cracker crumbs	375 mL
3 tbsp	unsalted butter, melted	45 mL

FILLING

1	packet (¼ oz/7.5 g) powdered unflavored gelatin	1
½ cup	Irish whiskey or bourbon	125 mL
2	packages (each 8 oz/250 g) cream cheese, softened	2
1 cup	granulated sugar	250 mL
2 tbsp	unsweetened cocoa powder, sifted	25 mL
1 tbsp	fresh lemon juice	15 mL
2 tsp	vanilla	10 mL
1 cup	whipping (35%) cream, whipped	250 mL

DECORATION

	Classic Whipped Cream Topping (see recipe, page 172)	
1 tbsp	unsweetened cocoa powder, sifted	15 mL

1. CRUST: In a medium bowl, combine graham cracker crumbs and butter. Press into bottom of cheesecake pan and freeze.

2. FILLING: Sprinkle gelatin over whiskey in a small saucepan and let stand for 1 minute. Stir over low heat until gelatin is completely dissolved (see Tip, left). Set aside to cool slightly. In a mixer bowl, beat cream cheese, sugar and cocoa powder on medium speed for 3 minutes. Slowly add dissolved gelatin. Mix in lemon juice and vanilla. Fold in whipped cream. Pour over frozen crust. Chill until firm, about 6 hours. Run a hot knife around edge of pan to loosen.

3. DECORATE: Ice top of cake with Classic Whipped Cream Topping or pipe rosettes around top of cake, if desired. Dust with a sprinkling of cocoa powder.

A *hint of whiskey will warm you up on a cold winter day.* ❧

SERVES 10 TO 12

TIP
Alcohol ignites easily, so use caution in warming the liquid to dissolve the gelatin.

VARIATION
Use cold coffee instead of the whiskey, if desired.

Lime

CHEESECAKE ❧

9-inch (23 cm) cheesecake pan, ungreased, or springform pan with 3-inch (7.5 cm) sides, greased (for other pan sizes, see page 10)

When traveling in Florida, my friend Neil and I came across a tart cheesecake. This perfect cool lime cheesecake is reminiscent of that delectable find.

❧

SERVES 10 TO 12

TIP
Zest limes before juicing. Leftover zest and juice freezes well for future recipes.

CRUST

1 1/4 cups	butter cookie crumbs	300 mL
3 tbsp	unsalted butter, melted	45 mL

FILLING

1	packet (1/4 oz/7.5 g) powdered unflavored gelatin	1
1/4 tsp	lime zest (see Tip, left)	1 mL
1/2 cup	fresh lime juice	125 mL
3	packages (each 8 oz/250 g) cream cheese, softened	3
3/4 cup	granulated sugar	175 mL
1 tsp	vanilla	5 mL
1 cup	whipping (35%) cream, whipped	250 mL

DECORATION

	Classic Whipped Cream Topping (see recipe, page 172)	
1/4 tsp	lime zest	1 mL

1. **CRUST:** In a medium bowl, combine cookie crumbs and butter. Press into bottom of cheesecake pan and freeze.

2. **FILLING:** Sprinkle gelatin over lime juice in a small saucepan and let stand for 1 minute. Stir over low heat until gelatin is completely dissolved. Set aside to cool slightly. In a mixer bowl, beat cream cheese and sugar on medium speed for 3 minutes. Slowly add dissolved gelatin. Mix in vanilla and lime zest. Fold in whipped cream. Pour over frozen crust. Chill until firm, about 6 hours. Run a hot knife around edge of pan to loosen.

3. **DECORATION:** Ice top of cake with Classic Whipped Cream Topping or pipe rosettes around top of cake, if desired. Sprinkle lime zest on top.

Mint

C H E E S E C A K E ❧

Mint is a flavor
that refreshes with
every bite. Try this
cheesecake with
an espresso.

❧

SERVES 10 TO 12

VARIATION
Substitute 1 tbsp
(15 mL) Crème
de Mint liqueur for
the mint extract.

*9-inch (23 cm) cheesecake pan, ungreased, or springform pan
with 3-inch (7.5 cm) sides, greased (for other pan sizes, see page 10)*

CRUST

1 1/4 cups	chocolate cookie crumbs	300 mL
3 tbsp	unsalted butter, melted	45 mL

FILLING

2	packets (each 1/4 oz/7.5 g) powdered unflavored gelatin	2
1/4 cup	cold water	50 mL
4	packages (each 8 oz/250 g) cream cheese, softened	4
1 cup	granulated sugar	250 mL
1/2 cup	milk	125 mL
1 tsp	vanilla	5 mL
1/4 tsp	mint extract	1 mL
2 cups	whipping (35%) cream, whipped	500 mL
6 oz	milk chocolate chunks	175 g

DECORATION

	Classic Whipped Cream Topping (see recipe, page 172)	
6	sprigs mint leaves	6

1. CRUST: In a medium bowl, combine cookie crumbs and butter. Press into bottom of cheesecake pan and freeze.

2. FILLING: Sprinkle gelatin over water in a small saucepan and let stand for 1 minute. Stir over low heat until gelatin is completely dissolved. Set aside to cool slightly. In a mixer bowl, beat cream cheese and sugar on medium speed for 3 minutes. Slowly add dissolved gelatin. Mix in milk, vanilla and mint extract. Fold in whipped cream and chocolate pieces. Pour over frozen crust. Chill until firm, about 6 hours. Run a hot knife around edge of pan to loosen.

3. DECORATION: Ice top of cake with Classic Whipped Cream Topping or pipe rosettes around top of cake, if desired. Garnish with mint leaves.

Nut Cheesecakes

Buckeye

C H E E S E C A K E

Preheat oven to 350°F (180°C)
9-inch (23 cm) cheesecake pan, ungreased, or springform pan
with 3-inch (7.5 cm) sides, greased (for other pan sizes, see page 10)

I was introduced to buckeyes, great chocolate candies packed with peanut butter, on my first teaching trip to Ohio. They inspired this cheesecake.

SERVES 10 TO 12

TIP
To melt chocolate in the microwave, break into squares and place in a microwave-safe dish. Microwave on high power for 1 to 2 minutes, stirring the mixture after 30 seconds.

VARIATION
Grate bittersweet chocolate on top of each individual serving.

CRUST

1½ cups	peanut butter sandwich cookie crumbs	375 mL
¼ cup	all-purpose flour	50 mL
¼ cup	unsalted butter, melted	50 mL

FILLING

4 oz	bittersweet chocolate, chopped	125 g
¼ cup	creamy peanut butter	50 mL
3	packages (each 8 oz/250 g) cream cheese, softened	3
1 cup	sour cream	250 mL
1½ cups	granulated sugar	375 mL
4	eggs	4
1 tsp	vanilla	5 mL

TOPPING

½ cup	sour cream	125 mL
¼ cup	granulated sugar	50 mL
¼ cup	creamy peanut butter	50 mL
1 tbsp	fresh lemon juice	15 mL
½ tsp	vanilla	2 mL

1. CRUST: In a medium bowl, combine cookie crumbs, flour and butter. Press into bottom of cheesecake pan and freeze.

2. FILLING: Melt chocolate in the top of a double boiler. When fully melted, add peanut butter and stir until blended. Set aside to cool slightly. In a large bowl, beat cream cheese, sour cream and sugar on medium-high speed for 3 minutes. Add eggs, one at a time, beating after each addition. Stir in vanilla. Swirl melted chocolate mixture into batter. Pour over frozen crust. Bake for 45 to 55 minutes or until the top is light brown and the center has a slight jiggle to it. Cool on the counter for 10 minutes (do not turn the oven off). The cake will sink slightly.

3. TOPPING: In a small bowl, combine sour cream, sugar, peanut butter, lemon juice and vanilla. Pour mixture into center of cooled cake; spread out to edges. Bake for 5 minutes more. Cool on a rack for 2 hours. Cover and refrigerate for at least 6 hours before serving.

Fresh Raspberry Hazelnut

CHEESECAKE

Preheat oven to 350°F (180°C)
9-inch (23 cm) cheesecake pan, ungreased, or springform pan with 3-inch (7.5 cm) sides, greased (for other pan sizes, see page 10)

> Fresh raspberries and toasted hazelnuts are a taste sensation!

SERVES 10 TO 12

TIP
If you can't find hazelnuts, you can use almonds instead.

VARIATION
Hazelnut liqueur adds another dimension of nutty flavor. Add 2 tbsp (25 mL) when you add vanilla, but don't eliminate any of the other liquids.

CRUST

1 1/4 cups	sugar cookie crumbs	300 mL
1/2 cup	hazelnuts, toasted and coarsely ground	125 mL
3 tbsp	unsalted butter, melted	45 mL

FILLING

4	packages (each 8 oz/250 g) cream cheese, softened	4
3/4 cup	sour cream	175 mL
1 1/4 cups	granulated sugar	300 mL
4	eggs	4
1/4 cup	all-purpose flour	50 mL
2 1/2 tbsp	fresh lemon juice	32 mL
1 tbsp	vanilla	15 mL
1 cup	raspberries, cut into quarters, if large	250 mL
1/2 cup	hazelnuts, toasted and coarsely ground	125 mL

TOPPING

1/2 cup	raspberries, whole	125 mL
1/4 cup	hazelnuts, toasted and chopped	50 mL
	Whipped cream, optional	

1. CRUST: In a medium bowl, combine cookie crumbs, hazelnuts and butter. Press into bottom of cheesecake pan and freeze.

2. FILLING: In a large bowl, beat cream cheese, sour cream and sugar on medium high for 3 minutes. Add eggs, one at a time, beating after each addition. Mix in flour, lemon juice and vanilla. Fold in raspberries and nuts. Pour batter over crust. Bake in preheated oven for 45 to 55 minutes or until the top is light brown. Cool for 2 hours. Cover with plastic wrap and refrigerate for 6 hours before decorating.

3. DECORATION: Sprinkle top with raspberries and nuts prior to serving. You can serve with a dollop of whipped cream on the side, if desired.

Creamy Peanut
CHEESECAKE ❧

Preheat oven to 350°F (180°C)
9-inch (23 cm) cheesecake pan, ungreased, or springform pan
with 3-inch (7.5 cm) sides, greased (for other pan sizes, see page 10)

This cheesecake is full of dry-roasted peanuts. Even though it's incredibly rich, don't skip the peanut butter whipped cream for the top, which adds an essential silky peanut finish. ❧

SERVES 10 TO 12

TIP

For the whipped cream to maintain its delicate texture and be firm enough to use in a pastry bag, extra flavorings, such as peanut butter, need to be added in small quantities first to lighten the flavorings. Whipped cream can be prepared and refrigerated for 2 hours before serving. Any liquid that forms can be whipped back into the mixture or discarded.

CRUST

1½ cups	peanut butter sandwich cookie crumbs	375 mL
¼ cup	all-purpose flour	50 mL
¼ cup	unsalted butter, melted	50 mL

FILLING

4	packages (each 8 oz/250 g) cream cheese, softened	4
8 oz	small curd cottage cheese, drained (see Tip, right)	250 g
1¼ cups	granulated sugar	300 mL
1 cup	creamy peanut butter	250 mL
4	eggs	4
3 tbsp	fresh lemon juice	45 mL
1 tsp	vanilla	5 mL
1 cup	dry-roasted peanuts, chopped	250 mL

TOPPING

½ cup	sour cream	125 mL
¼ cup	granulated sugar	50 mL
¼ cup	creamy peanut butter	50 mL
1 tbsp	fresh lemon juice	15 mL
½ tsp	vanilla	2 mL

DECORATION

1 cup	whipping (35%) cream	250 mL
2 tbsp	granulated sugar	25 mL
2 tbsp	creamy peanut butter	25 mL

1. CRUST: In a medium bowl, combine cookie crumbs, flour and butter. Press into bottom of cheesecake pan and freeze.

2. FILLING: In a large mixer bowl, beat cream cheese, cottage cheese and sugar on medium-high speed for 3 minutes. Blend in peanut butter on medium-high speed for 2 minutes. Add eggs, one at a time, beating after each addition. Stir in lemon juice and vanilla. With a rubber spatula, stir in peanuts. Pour over frozen crust. Bake in preheated oven for 45 to 55 minutes or until the top is light brown and the center has a slight jiggle to it. Cool on the counter for 10 minutes (do not turn the oven off). The cake will sink slightly.

3. TOPPING: In a small bowl, combine sour cream, sugar, peanut butter, lemon juice and vanilla. Pour mixture into center of cooled cake and spread out to edges. Bake for 5 minutes more. Cool on a rack for 2 hours. Cover and refrigerate for at least 6 hours before decorating or serving.

4. DECORATION: In a well-chilled bowl, whip cream on medium-high speed until soft peaks form. With the mixer still running, sprinkle sugar into cream and continue whipping until firm peaks form. Remove $\frac{1}{2}$ cup (125 mL) cream and stir into peanut butter. Fold cream and peanut butter mixture into whipped cream. Ice top of cooled caked or pipe a border around top of cake.

Peanut Brittle

CHEESECAKE ❧

SERVES 10 TO 12

TIP
Use fresh peanut brittle, which is easy to find at holiday time.

VARIATION
If you can find other brittle, such as almond or macadamia, use by all means.

Preheat oven to 350°F (180°C)
9-inch (23 cm) cheesecake pan, ungreased, or springform pan with 3-inch (7.5 cm) sides, greased (for other pan sizes, see page 10)

CRUST

1½ cups	butter cookie crumbs	375 mL
¼ cup	unsalted butter, melted	50 mL

FILLING

4	packages (each 8 oz/250 g) cream cheese, softened	4
1¼ cups	granulated sugar	300 mL
4	eggs	4
1 cup	sour cream	250 mL
¼ cup	all-purpose flour	50 mL
1 tbsp	vanilla	15 mL
3 oz	peanut brittle, crushed into bite-size pieces	90 g

DECORATION

	Classic Whipped Cream Topping (see recipe, page 172)	
3 oz	peanut brittle	90 g

1. CRUST: In a medium bowl, combine cookie crumbs and butter. Press into bottom of cheesecake pan and freeze.

2. FILLING: In a large mixer bowl, beat cream cheese and sugar on medium-high speed for 3 minutes. Add eggs, one at a time, beating after each addition. Mix in sour cream, flour and vanilla. Fold in peanut brittle. Pour batter over frozen crust. Bake in preheated oven for 45 to 55 minutes or until the top is light brown and the center has a slight jiggle to it. Cool on a rack for 2 hours. Cover with plastic wrap and refrigerate for at least 6 hours before decorating or serving.

3. DECORATION: Ice top of cake with Classic Whipped Cream Topping or pipe rosettes around top of cake, if desired. Top with pieces of peanut brittle.

Peanut Butter

CHEESECAKE

SERVES 10 TO 12

TIP
Use a commercial creamy peanut butter. The natural peanut butters have too much oil for this recipe.

VARIATION
Omit the sour cream topping. Sprinkle top with ½ cup (125 mL) semi-sweet chocolate chips instead.

Preheat oven to 350°F (180°C)
9-inch (23 cm) cheesecake pan, ungreased, or springform pan with 3-inch (7.5 cm) sides, greased (for other pan sizes, see page 10)

CRUST

1½ cups	peanut butter sandwich cookie crumbs	375 mL
¼ cup	dry-roasted peanuts, crushed	50 mL
¼ cup	all-purpose flour	50 mL
¼ cup	unsalted butter, melted	50 mL

FILLING

3	packages (each 8 oz/250 g) cream cheese, softened	3
1 cup	sour cream	250 mL
¼ cup	creamy peanut butter	50 mL
1½ cups	granulated sugar	375 mL
4	eggs	4
1 tsp	vanilla	5 mL

TOPPING

½ cup	sour cream	125 mL
¼ cup	granulated sugar	50 mL
¼ cup	creamy peanut butter	50 mL
1 tbsp	fresh lemon juice	15 mL
½ tsp	vanilla	2 mL
¼ cup	dry-roasted peanuts	50 mL

1. CRUST: In a medium bowl, combine cookie crumbs, flour, peanuts and butter. Press into bottom of cheesecake pan and freeze.

2. FILLING: In a large mixer bowl, beat cream cheese, sour cream, peanut butter and sugar on medium-high speed for 3 minutes. Add eggs, one at a time, beating after each addition. Stir in vanilla. Pour over frozen crust. Bake in preheated oven for 45 to 55 minutes or until the top is light brown and the center has a slight jiggle to it. Cool on the counter for 10 minutes (do not turn the oven off). The cake will sink slightly.

3. TOPPING: In a small bowl, combine sour cream, sugar, peanut butter, lemon juice and vanilla. Pour mixture into center of cooled cake and spread out to edges. Sprinkle top with peanuts. Bake for 5 minutes more. Cool on a rack for 2 hours. Cover and refrigerate for at least 6 hours before serving.

Hazelnut

CHEESECAKE ❧

Preheat oven to 350°F (180°C)
9-inch (23 cm) cheesecake pan, ungreased, or springform pan
with 3-inch (7.5 cm) sides, greased (for other pan sizes, see page 10)

> Hazelnuts, once only available at holiday time, are now easy to find year-round. This simple cheesecake lets the hazelnut flavor shine through. ❧

SERVES 10 TO 12

TIP
To toast hazelnuts, place in a preheated 350ºF (180ºC) oven for 10 to 12 minutes, stirring a few times until lightly browned and fragrant. You can use them with the skins on, if desired.

VARIATION
A few slices of fresh fruit on each serving plate will turn this dessert into a cheese course — it's rich, but not too sweet.

CRUST

1 ½ cups	butter cookie crumbs	375 mL
¼ cup	unsalted butter, melted	50 mL

FILLING

3	packages (each 8 oz/250 g) cream cheese, softened	3
8 oz	small curd cottage cheese, drained (see Tip, page 36)	250 g
1 cup	plain yogurt	250 mL
1 ¼ cups	granulated sugar	300 mL
2	eggs	2
2	egg yolks	2
3 tbsp	fresh lemon juice	45 mL
1 tsp	vanilla	5 mL
1 cup	hazelnuts, toasted and chopped	250 mL

DECORATION

1 cup	Classic Whipped Cream Topping (see recipe, page 172)	

1. CRUST: In a medium bowl, combine cookie crumbs and butter. Press into bottom of cheesecake pan and freeze.

2. FILLING: In a large mixer bowl, beat cream cheese, cottage cheese, yogurt and sugar on medium-high speed for 3 minutes. Add eggs and egg yolks, one at a time, beating after each addition. Mix in lemon juice and vanilla. With a rubber spatula, stir in hazelnuts. Pour batter over frozen crust. Bake in preheated oven for 45 to 55 minutes or until the top is light brown and the center has a slight jiggle to it. Cool on a rack for 2 hours. Cover with plastic wrap and refrigerate for at least 6 hours before decorating or serving.

3. DECORATION: Ice top of cooled cake with Classic Whipped Cream Topping or pipe a border around top of cake, if desired.

Kentucky Bourbon

CHEESECAKE

SERVES 10 TO 12

TIP
Save time by purchasing blanched, skinless almonds to toast. Save money by purchasing them with the skins on, which
can be removed by rubbing them in a dishtowel while still hot from toasting.

VARIATION
Pecan is another nut that goes well with Kentucky flavors.

Preheat oven to 350°F (180°C)
9-inch (23 cm) cheesecake pan, ungreased, or springform pan
with 3-inch (7.5 cm) sides, greased (for other pan sizes, see page 10)

CRUST

1½ cups	almonds, toasted and ground	375 mL
¼ cup	all-purpose flour	50 mL
¼ cup	unsalted butter, melted	50 mL

FILLING

4	packages (each 8 oz/250 g) cream cheese, softened	4
1¼ cups	granulated sugar	300 mL
2	eggs	2
3	egg yolks	3
3 tbsp	Kentucky Bourbon	45 mL
1 cup	chopped almonds	250 mL
1 tsp	vanilla	5 mL

DECORATION

Classic Whipped Cream Topping
(see recipe, page 172)

1. CRUST: In a medium bowl, combine almonds, flour and butter. Press into bottom of cheesecake pan and freeze.

2. FILLING: In a large mixer bowl, beat cream cheese and sugar on medium-high speed for 3 minutes. Add eggs and egg yolks, one at a time, beating after each addition. Fold in bourbon, chopped almonds and vanilla. Pour batter over frozen crust. Bake in preheated oven for 45 to 55 minutes or until the top is light brown and the center has a slight jiggle to it. Cool on a rack for 2 hours. Cover with plastic wrap and refrigerate for at least 6 hours before decorating or serving.

3. DECORATION: Ice top of cake with Classic Whipped Cream Topping, if desired.

Pecan Praline

CHESECAKE

I *love pralines and cream ice cream, so wouldn't it be great as a cheesecake?*

SERVES 10 TO 12

TIP
You can make the glazed pecans weeks ahead. Just store in an airtight container. I also like to use the pecans in salads with a blue cheese crumble and oil and vinegar dressing.

VARIATION
Use all the glazed pecans in the filling. Ice top of cake with whipped cream. Sprinkle with chopped pecans.

Preheat oven to 350°F (180°C)
9-inch (23 cm) cheesecake pan, ungreased, or springform pan with 3-inch (7.5 cm) sides, greased (for other pan sizes, see page 10)
13-by 9-inch (3 L) baking pan, lined with parchment paper

CRUST

1¼ cups	pecans, coarsely ground	300 mL
¼ cup	all-purpose flour	50 mL
3 tbsp	unsalted butter	45 mL

FILLING

1	egg white	1
¼ cup	granulated sugar	50 mL
1½ cups	pecan halves	375 mL
4 oz	cream cheese, softened	125 g
½ cup	liquid honey	125 mL
2 cups	ricotta cheese, drained (see Tip, page 25)	500 mL
2	eggs	2
1 tsp	vanilla	5 mL
½ cup	plain yogurt	125 mL
⅓ cup	cornstarch	75 mL

DECORATION

Classic Whipped Cream Topping (see recipe, page 172)

1. **CRUST:** In a medium bowl, combine pecans, flour and butter. Press into bottom of cheesecake pan and freeze.

2. **FILLING:** In a bowl, whisk egg white and sugar. Add pecans, stirring to coat evenly. Spread out evenly on prepared baking pan. Bake for 10 to 18 minutes or until light brown. Reserve 12 pecans for decorating; break up remaining pecans. Set aside.

3. In a large bowl, beat cream cheese, honey and ricotta on medium high for 3 minutes. Add eggs, one at a time, beating after each addition. Mix in vanilla. Stir in yogurt and cornstarch. Gently fold in broken pecans. Pour over frozen crust. Bake for 45 to 55 minutes or until the top is light brown. Cool for 2 hours. Cover and refrigerate for 6 hours.

4. **DECORATION:** Ice top of cake with Classic Whipped Cream Topping or pipe rosettes around top of cake, if desired. Top with reserved glazed pecans.

Pistachio

C H E E S E C A K E

Preheat oven to 350°F (180°C)
9-inch (23 cm) cheesecake pan, ungreased, or springform pan
with 3-inch (7.5 cm) sides, greased (for other pan sizes, see page 10)

P*istachios are a great addition to cheesecakes — both in the filling and as decoration.*

SERVES 10 TO 12

TIP
Use fresh lime juice instead of bottled, which sometimes has a metallic taste.

VARIATIONS
Garnish each slice with Fresh Raspberry Sauce (see recipe, page 174) during the holidays for a green and red effect.

Use chocolate sandwich cookies instead of the butter ones for the crust. It's a delicious alternative.

CRUST

1½ cups	butter cookie crumbs	375 mL
¼ cup	unsalted butter, melted	50 mL

FILLING

2	packages (each 8 oz/250 g) cream cheese, softened	2
2 cups	ricotta cheese, drained (see Tip, page 25)	500 mL
1 cup	sour cream	250 mL
1½ cups	granulated sugar	375 mL
5	eggs	5
1 cup	pistachios, ground fine	250 mL
½ cup	all-purpose flour	125 mL
2 tbsp	fresh lime juice	25 mL
1 tbsp	vanilla	15 mL

DECORATION

	Classic Whipped Cream Topping (see recipe, page 172)	
¼ cup	ground pistachios	50 mL

1. CRUST: In a medium bowl, combine cookie crumbs and butter. Press into bottom of cheesecake pan and freeze.

2. FILLING: In a large mixer bowl, beat cream cheese, ricotta, sour cream and sugar on medium-high speed for 3 minutes. Add eggs, one at a time, beating after each addition. Stir in pistachios, flour, lime juice and vanilla. Pour batter over frozen crust. Bake in preheated oven for 45 to 55 minutes or until the top is light brown and the center has a slight jiggle to it. Cool on a rack for 2 hours. Cover with plastic wrap and refrigerate for at least 6 hours before decorating or serving.

3. DECORATION: Ice top of cake with Classic Whipped Cream Topping or pipe rosettes around top of cake, if desired. Top with a dusting of pistachios.

Toasted Almond

CHEESECAKE

SERVES 10 TO 12

TIP
Prepare cookie crumbs quickly in a food processor, fitted with a metal blade, by pulsing whole cookies on and off a few
times. When mixed with the butter, the crumbs should feel like wet sand.

VARIATIONS
Orange-flavored liqueurs are a good flavor accent to the almonds. A non-alcoholic substitute is orange juice concentrate.

Preheat oven to 350°F (180°C)
9-inch (23 cm) cheesecake pan, ungreased, or springform pan with 3-inch (7.5 cm) sides, greased (for other pan sizes, see page 10)

CRUST

1 1/2 cups	almond cookie crumbs	375 mL
1/4 cup	unsalted butter, melted	50 mL

FILLING

4	packages (each 8 oz/250 g) cream cheese, softened	4
1 1/4 cups	granulated sugar	300 mL
4	eggs	4
2 tbsp	instant coffee powder	25 mL
1 tbsp	hot water	15 mL
3 tbsp	almond-flavored liqueur	45 mL
1/2 cup	almonds, toasted and chopped	125 mL
1 tsp	vanilla	5 mL

DECORATION

	Classic Whipped Cream Topping (see recipe, page 172)	
12	whole almonds, toasted	12

1. CRUST: In a medium bowl, combine cookie crumbs and butter. Press into bottom of cheesecake pan and freeze.

2. FILLING: In a large mixer bowl, beat cream cheese and sugar on medium-high speed for 3 minutes. Add eggs, one at a time, beating after each addition. In a small bowl, dissolve coffee powder in hot water. Stir into cheese mixture. Add almond liqueur, chopped almonds and vanilla. Pour batter over frozen crust. Bake in preheated oven for 45 to 55 minutes or until the top is light brown and the center has a slight jiggle to it. Cool on a rack for 2 hours. Cover with plastic wrap and refrigerate for at least 6 hours before decorating or serving.

3. DECORATION: Ice top of cake with Classic Whipped Cream Topping or pipe rosettes around top of cake, if desired. Top with whole almonds.

Toasted Pecan

CHESECAKE

When teaching in Whistler during the spring one year a student proclaimed that this cheesecake should be proclaimed a national treasure.

SERVES 10 TO 12

TIP
Store raw nuts in the freezer and toast them right before using.

VARIATION
For the garnish, substitute 12 glazed pecans (see Pecan Praline Cheesecake, page 114).

Preheat oven to 350°F (180°C)
9-inch (23 cm) cheesecake pan, ungreased, or springform pan
with 3-inch (7.5 cm) sides, greased (for other pan sizes, see page 10)

CRUST

1½ cups	pecans, toasted and coarsely ground	375 mL
¼ cup	all-purpose flour	50 mL
¼ cup	unsalted butter, melted	50 mL

FILLING

3	packages (each 8 oz/250 g) cream cheese, softened	3
1 cup	plain yogurt	250 mL
1¼ cups	granulated sugar	300 mL
4	eggs	4
1 cup	chopped pecans	250 mL
1 tsp	vanilla	5 mL

DECORATION

	Classic Whipped Cream Topping (see recipe, page 172)	
¼ cup	chopped pecans	50 mL

1. CRUST: In a medium bowl, combine pecans, flour and butter. Press into bottom of cheesecake pan and freeze.

2. FILLING: In a large mixer bowl, beat cream cheese, yogurt and sugar on medium-high speed for 3 minutes. Add eggs, one at a time, beating after each addition. Fold in pecans and vanilla. Pour batter over frozen crust. Bake in preheated oven for 45 to 55 minutes or until the top is light brown and the center has a slight jiggle to it. Cool on a rack for 2 hours. Cover with plastic wrap and refrigerate for at least 6 hours before decorating or serving.

3. DECORATING: Ice top of cake with Classic Whipped Cream Topping, if desired. Sprinkle with chopped pecans.

Walnut Date

CHEESECAKE

SERVES 10 TO 12

VARIATION
Substitute chopped
prunes instead of
dates if you have
them on hand.

Preheat oven to 350°F (180°C)
9-inch (23 cm) cheesecake pan, ungreased, or springform pan
with 3-inch (7.5 cm) sides, greased (for other pan sizes, see page 10)

CRUST

1½ cups	walnuts, toasted and ground	375 mL
¼ cup	all-purpose flour	50 mL
¼ cup	unsalted butter, melted	50 mL

FILLING

3	packages (each 8 oz/250 g) cream cheese, softened	3
1 cup	sour cream	250 mL
¼ cup	liquid honey	50 mL
1¼ cups	granulated sugar	300 mL
4	eggs	4
1 cup	chopped walnuts	250 mL
½ cup	chopped dates, pitted	125 mL
1 tsp	vanilla	5 mL

DECORATION

	Classic Whipped Cream Topping (see recipe, page 172)	
¼ cup	whole walnuts	50 mL

1. CRUST: In a medium bowl, combine walnuts, flour and butter. Press into bottom of cheesecake pan and freeze.

2. FILLING: In a large mixer bowl, beat cream cheese, sour cream, honey and sugar on medium-high speed for 3 minutes. Add eggs, one at a time, beating after each addition. Fold in walnuts, dates and vanilla. Pour batter over frozen crust. Bake in preheated oven for 45 to 55 minutes or until the top is light brown and the center has a slight jiggle to it. Cool on a rack for 2 hours. Cover with plastic wrap and refrigerate for at least 6 hours before decorating or serving.

3. DECORATION: Ice top of cake with Classic Whipped Cream Topping, if desired. Sprinkle with whole walnuts.

Mini-Cheesecakes and Bars

Almond

MINI-CHEESECAKE

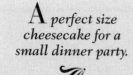
SERVES 4 TO 6

TIP
To be economical, purchase almonds whole with the skins on. To toast, place in a preheated 350°F (180°C) oven for 10 to 12 minutes or until fragrant. Rub hot nuts in a dish-towel to remove the skins.
Don't chop nuts until they have cooled.

VARIATION
For an even silkier texture, use mascarpone instead of regular cream cheese.

Preheat oven to 300°F (150°C)
6-inch (15 cm) cheesecake, ungreased, or springform pan, greased (for other pan size, see page 10)

CRUST

¾ cup	almond cookie crumbs	175 mL
2 tbsp	unsalted butter, melted	25 mL

FILLING

2	packages (each 8 oz/250 g) cream cheese, softened	2
¾ cup	granulated sugar	175 mL
2	eggs	2
2 tbsp	almond-flavored liqueur	25 mL
¼ cup	chopped almonds	50 mL
1 tsp	vanilla	5 mL

DECORATION

	Classic Whipped Cream Topping (see recipe, page 172)	
6	whole almonds	6

1. CRUST: In a medium bowl, combine cookie crumbs and butter. Press into bottom of cheesecake pan and freeze.

2. FILLING: In a large mixer bowl, beat cream cheese and sugar on medium-high speed for 3 minutes. Add eggs, one at a time, beating after each addition. Add liqueur, chopped almonds and vanilla. Pour over frozen crust. Bake for 22 to 30 minutes or until the top is light brown and the center has a slight jiggle to it. Cool completely on a wire rack. Cover and refrigerate for 4 hours or overnight before decorating and serving.

3. DECORATION: Ice top of cake with Classic Whipped Cream Topping or pipe rosettes around top of cake, if desired. Top with whole almonds.

Dutch Apple

CHEESECAKE SQUARES ❧

These cheesecake bars are very rich with crisp apples lining the top and center.

❧

SERVES 18

TIPS

You can prepare these cheesecake bars up to 3 weeks prior to serving. Wrap the pan in plastic wrap and wrap again with foil, then freeze. Defrost in the refrigerator 24 hours before serving.

Good baking apples to use for this recipe are Granny Smith or pippin.

VARIATION

Mix the sliced apple topping into the batter in addition to the chopped apples.

Preheat oven to 325°F (160°C)
13-by 9-inch (3 L) baking pan, lined with foil, sprayed with nonstick spray

CRUST

2 ½ cups	graham cracker crumbs	625 mL
½ cup	unsalted butter, melted	125 mL

FILLING

3	packages (each 8 oz/250 g) cream cheese, softened	3
1 cup	sour cream	250 mL
1 ½ cups	packed light brown sugar	375 mL
4	eggs	4
1 tbsp	vanilla	15 mL
1 tsp	fresh lemon juice	5 mL
1 tsp	ground cinnamon	5 mL
½ tsp	fresh ground nutmeg	2 mL
¼ tsp	ground cloves	1 mL
1	medium baking apple, peeled and finely chopped	1

TOPPING

3 tbsp	unsalted butter, cold	45 mL
¼ cup	all-purpose flour	50 mL
¼ cup	packed light brown sugar	50 mL
½ tsp	ground cinnamon	2 mL
¼ tsp	ground cloves	1 mL
12	thin apple slices, about 1 medium apple	12

1. CRUST: In a bowl, combine graham cracker crumbs and butter. Press into baking pan and freeze.

2. FILLING: In a large mixer bowl, beat cream cheese, sour cream and brown sugar on medium-high speed for 3 minutes. Add eggs, one at a time, beating after each addition. Mix in vanilla and lemon juice. Mix in cinnamon, nutmeg and cloves. Fold in chopped apple. Pour over frozen crust.

3. TOPPING: In a bowl, cut butter into flour. Add sugar, cinnamon and cloves. Toss in apples. Arrange mixture in a spiral over batter. Bake for 40 to 50 minutes or until apples are light brown and firm in center. Cool for 2 hours. Refrigerate 6 hours before cutting into squares.

Mini-Lemon

CHEESECAKES

MAKES 16 OR 24 MINI-CHEESE-CAKES

TIPS
To freeze, cool completely. Wrap each cake in plastic wrap, then wrap again in foil.

You can divide this recipe in half and make 12 mini cheesecakes using a regular-size muffin tin.

VARIATION
Add up to 1 tbsp (15 mL) jam on top of each cake and create an array of flavors.

Preheat oven to 300°F (150°C)
Texas-size muffin tins with at least 16 cups (about 1⁵⁄₈ inches/ 4 cm deep) or 24 regular-size muffin cups (about 1¼ inches/ 3 cm deep), lined with paper muffin cups

CRUST

2½ cups	graham cracker crumbs	625 mL
½ cup	unsalted butter, melted	125 mL

FILLING

4	packages (each 8 oz/250 g) cream cheese, softened	4
1¼ cups	granulated sugar	300 mL
4	eggs	4
3 tbsp	fresh lemon juice	45 mL
1 tsp	vanilla	5 mL

TOPPING

1 cup	sour cream	250 mL
½ cup	granulated sugar	125 mL
1 tbsp	fresh lemon juice	15 mL
1 tsp	vanilla	5 mL

1. CRUST: In a medium bowl, combine graham cracker crumbs and butter. Press into bottom of prepared muffin cups and freeze.

2. FILLING: In a large mixer bowl, beat cream cheese and sugar on medium-high speed for 3 minutes. Add eggs, one at a time, beating after each addition. Mix in lemon juice and vanilla. Fill each cup about three-quarters full. Bake for 20 to 25 minutes or until they look puffy and the centers have a slight jiggle. Cool on a rack for 10 minutes (do not turn the oven off).

3. TOPPING: In a small bowl, combine sour cream, sugar, lemon juice and vanilla. Pour mixture into the center of each cooled cake and spread out to edges. Bake for 5 minutes more. Cool on a rack for 2 hours. Cover and refrigerate for at least 6 hours before serving.

Grasshopper
CHEESE BARS ❧

No grasshoppers in this cheesecake — just the cool sensation of chocolate and mint.

❧

SERVES 12 TO 18

VARIATION
Substitute mint chips for the semi-sweet chocolate and omit peppermint extract.

Preheat oven to 325°F (160°C)
13-by 9-inch (3 L) baking pan, lined with foil,
sprayed with nonstick spray

CRUST

2¼ cups	chocolate sandwich cookie crumbs	550 mL
⅓ cup	unsalted butter, melted	75 mL

FILLING

3	packages (each 8 oz/250 g) cream cheese, softened	3
¾ cup	granulated sugar	175 mL
3	eggs	3
¼ cup	all-purpose flour	50 mL
½ cup	sour cream	125 mL
1 tsp	vanilla	5 mL
¼ tsp	peppermint extract	1 mL
3 oz	semi-sweet chocolate, melted and cooled	90 g

DECORATION

Classic Whipped Cream Topping
(see recipe, page 172)

1. CRUST: In a medium bowl, combine cookie crumbs and butter. Press into bottom of prepared pan and freeze.

2. FILLING: In a large mixer bowl, beat cream cheese and sugar on medium-high speed for 3 minutes. Add eggs, one at a time, beating after each addition. Mix in flour, sour cream, vanilla and peppermint. With the mixer still running, pour in the melted and cooled semi-sweet chocolate in a steady stream. Pour batter over frozen crust. Bake in preheated oven for 45 to 55 minutes or until the top is light brown and the center has a slight jiggle to it. Cool on a rack for 2 hours. Cover with plastic wrap and refrigerate for at least 6 hours before decorating or cutting into bars.

3. DECORATION: Cut into bars or squares. Top each with whipped cream, if desired.

Chocolate Peanut Butter

CHEESE BARS ❧

SERVES 10 TO 12

TIP
Use a commercial creamy peanut butter. The natural peanut butters have too much oil for this recipe.

Preheat oven to 325°F (160°C)
13-by 9-inch (3 L) baking pan, lined with foil

CRUST

2½ cups	peanut butter sandwich cookie crumbs	625 mL
½ cup	all-purpose flour	125 mL
½ cup	unsalted butter, melted	125 mL

FILLING

4	packages (each 8 oz/250 g) cream cheese, softened	4
1¼ cups	granulated sugar	300 mL
4	eggs	4
1 cup	creamy peanut butter	250 mL
8 oz	bittersweet chocolate, melted and cooled	250 g
3 tbsp	fresh lemon juice	45 mL
1 tsp	vanilla	5 mL
2 cups	semi-sweet chocolate chunks	500 mL

TOPPING

1 cup	sour cream	250 mL
½ cup	granulated sugar	125 mL
⅓ cup	creamy peanut butter	75 mL
1 tbsp	fresh lemon juice	15 mL
1 tsp	vanilla	5 mL
½ cup	semi-sweet chocolate chunks	125 mL

VARIATION
You can use
milk chocolate
chunks instead of
semi-sweet chocolate
in the topping.

1. CRUST: In a medium bowl, combine cookie crumbs, flour and butter. Press into bottom of prepared baking pan and freeze.

2. FILLING: In a large mixer bowl, beat cream cheese and sugar on medium-high speed for 3 minutes. Add eggs, one at a time, beating after each addition. Blend in peanut butter and chocolate. Mix in lemon juice and vanilla. Fold in chocolate chunks. Pour over frozen crust. Bake for 35 to 45 minutes or until the top is light brown and the center has a slight jiggle to it. Cool on the counter for 10 minutes (do not turn the oven off). The cake will sink slightly.

3. TOPPING: In a small bowl, combine sour cream, sugar, peanut butter, lemon juice and vanilla. Pour into center of cooled cake and spread out to edges. Sprinkle with chocolate chunks. Bake for 5 minutes more. Cool on a rack for 2 hours. Cover and refrigerate for at least 6 hours before cutting into bars.

Quadruple-Chocolate

CHEESE BARS

SERVES 10 TO 12

TIP
Wrap each bar in plastic wrap to travel in a picnic or gift basket. To freeze, wrap foil around the plastic wrap and freeze for 3 to 4 months.

VARIATION
A chocolate sandwich cookie crust instead of the coarsely ground pecans will be popular with children of all ages.

Preheat oven to 325°F (160°C)
13-by 9-inch (3 L) baking pan, lined with foil, sprayed with nonstick spray

CRUST

2 cups	pecans, coarsely ground	500 mL
¼ cup	all-purpose flour	50 mL
¼ cup	unsalted butter, melted	50 mL

FILLING

¼ cup	unsweetened cocoa powder	50 mL
3 tbsp	hot water	45 mL
4	packages (each 8 oz/250 g) cream cheese, softened	4
1½ cups	granulated sugar	375 mL
5	eggs	5
2 tbsp	fresh lemon juice	25 mL
1 tsp	vanilla	5 mL
8 oz	bittersweet chocolate chunks	250 g
6 oz	white chocolate chunks	175 g
6 oz	milk chocolate chunks	175 g

1. CRUST: In a medium bowl, combine pecans, flour and butter. Press into bottom of prepared baking pan and bake in preheated oven for 12 minutes. Cool until filling is ready.

2. FILLING: In a small bowl, dissolve cocoa powder in hot water. Set aside. In a large mixer bowl, beat cream cheese and sugar on medium-high speed for 3 minutes. Add eggs, one at a time, beating after each addition. Mix in lemon juice and vanilla. With a rubber spatula, fold in cocoa mixture and chocolate chunks. Pour batter into baked crust. Bake in preheated oven for 25 to 30 minutes or until the top is light brown and the center has a slight jiggle to it. Cool on a rack for 2 hours before refrigerating. The top will sink slightly. Refrigerate for at least 6 hours before cutting into squares or bars.

Cheese Pies

Apple Nutmeg

CHEESE PIE

SERVES 5 TO 6

TIP
When cutting apples, soak the pieces in lemon juice and water while waiting for the rest of the recipe to be ready to keep them from turning brown. If you are out of lemons, you can break up a vita- min C tablet in the water.

VARIATION
For a different twist, use ripe pear instead of apple.

Preheat oven to 325°F (160°C)
9-inch (23 cm) pie plate, ungreased

CRUST

1 1/4 cups	butter cookie crumbs	300 mL
3 tbsp	unsalted butter, melted	45 mL
1 tsp	ground nutmeg	5 mL

FILLING

2	packages (each 8 oz/250 g) cream cheese, softened	2
1/4 cup	sour cream	50 mL
1/2 cup	packed light brown sugar	125 mL
2	eggs	2
1	medium baking apple, such as Granny Smith or pippin, peeled and diced	1
1 tsp	ground nutmeg	5 mL
1/2 tsp	ground cinnamon	2 mL
1/4 tsp	ground allspice	1 mL
1/2 tsp	vanilla	2 mL

1. **CRUST:** In a medium bowl, combine cookie crumbs, butter and nutmeg. Press into bottom and sides of pie plate and freeze.

2. **FILLING:** In a large mixer bowl, beat cream cheese, sour cream and brown sugar on medium-high speed for 3 minutes. Add eggs, one at a time, beating after each addition. Fold in diced apples, nutmeg, cinnamon, allspice and vanilla. Pour batter over frozen crust. Bake in preheated oven for 25 to 35 minutes or until the top is light brown and the center has a slight jiggle to it. Cool on a rack for 2 hours. Cover with plastic wrap and refrigerate for at least 6 hours before serving.

Berry Berry Berry Cheesecake (page 96)
Overleaf: Maple Pumpkin Cheesecake (page 153)

Banana Macadamia

CHEESE PIE

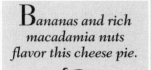
Bananas and rich macadamia nuts flavor this cheese pie.

SERVES 5 TO 6

TIP
Look for dried bananas in the health food section of your supermarket. If you use fresh bananas for decorating they will turn black before you can serve the dessert.

VARIATION
Pecans or hazelnuts are a less expensive substitute for macadamia nuts.

Preheat oven to 325°F (160°C)
9-inch (23 cm) pie plate, ungreased

CRUST

1¼ cups	graham cracker crumbs	300 mL
3 tbsp	unsalted butter, melted	45 mL

FILLING

2	packages (each 8 oz/250 g) cream cheese, softened	2
¾ cup	ripe mashed bananas, about 3 large	175 mL
½ cup	packed light brown sugar	125 mL
2	eggs	2
2 tbsp	all-purpose flour	25 mL
¼ cup	macadamia nuts, toasted and ground	50 mL
1 tsp	ground cinnamon	5 mL
½ tsp	ground nutmeg	2 mL
½ tsp	vanilla	2 mL

DECORATION

	Classic Whipped Cream Topping (see recipe, page 172)	
5 to 6	banana chips	5 to 6

1. CRUST: In a medium bowl, combine graham cracker crumbs and butter. Press into bottom and sides of pie plate and freeze.

2. FILLING: In a large mixer bowl, beat cream cheese, bananas and brown sugar on medium-high speed for 3 minutes. Add eggs, one at a time, beating after each addition. Fold in flour, macadamia nuts, cinnamon, nutmeg and vanilla. Pour batter over frozen crust. Bake in preheated oven for 25 to 35 minutes or until the top is light brown and the center has a slight jiggle to it. Cool on a rack for 2 hours. Cover with plastic wrap and refrigerate for at least 6 hours before decorating or serving.

3. DECORATION: Ice top of pie with Classic Whipped Cream Topping or pipe rosettes around top, if desired. Top with dried banana chips.

◄ Turtle Cheese Pie (page 132)
Overleaf: Cranberry Orange Cheesecake (page 157)

Chocolate Chunk

CHEESE PIE

*P ort would be
perfect served with
this rich pie.*

SERVES 5 TO 6

TIP
The crust needs to
cool completely
before filling it to
keep it crisp.

VARIATION
Use white chocolate
chunks instead of
the bittersweet for
a different look.

Preheat oven to 350°F (180°C)
9-inch (23 cm) pie plate, ungreased

CRUST

1 cup	pecans, coarsely ground	250 mL
3 tbsp	all-purpose flour	45 mL
2 tbsp	unsalted butter, melted	25 mL

FILLING

2 tbsp	unsweetened cocoa powder	25 mL
1½ tbsp	hot water	22 mL
2	packages (each 8 oz/250 g) cream cheese, softened	2
¾ cup	granulated sugar	175 mL
2	eggs	2
1 tbsp	fresh lemon juice	15 mL
1 tsp	vanilla	5 mL
4 oz	bittersweet chocolate chunks	125 g

DECORATION

1	Fresh Raspberry Sauce (see recipe, page 174)	1

1. CRUST: In a medium bowl, combine pecans, flour and butter. Press into bottom and sides of pie plate and bake in preheated oven for 6 minutes. Cool until filling is ready. Reduce oven temperature to 325°F (160°C).

2. FILLING: In a small bowl, dissolve cocoa powder in hot water. Set aside. In a large mixer bowl, beat cream cheese and sugar on medium-high speed for 3 minutes. Add eggs, one at a time, beating after each addition. Mix in lemon juice and vanilla. Using a rubber spatula, fold in cocoa mixture and chocolate chunks. Pour batter into baked crust. Bake in preheated oven for 22 to 30 minutes or until the top is light brown and the center has a slight jiggle to it. Cool on a rack for 2 hours. Cover with plastic wrap and refrigerate for at least 6 hours before decorating or serving.

3. DECORATION: Top each slice with a spoonful of Fresh Raspberry Sauce.

Brownie

CHEESE PIE ❧

Two layers, one a rich brownie, the other a sweet vanilla, make this a great choice for summer picnics. ❧

SERVES 5 TO 6

TIP
Having a second large mixer bowl saves washing dishes mid-recipe.

VARIATION
Top with Fresh Raspberry Sauce (see recipe, page 174).

Preheat oven to 325°F (160°C)
9-inch (23 cm) pie plate, ungreased

CRUST

1 cup	chocolate sandwich cookie crumbs	250 mL
3 tbsp	unsalted butter, melted	45 mL

FILLING

1/3 cup	unsalted butter, softened	75 mL
1/3 cup	granulated sugar	75 mL
2	eggs	2
1 1/4 tsp	vanilla	6 mL
1/8 tsp	salt	0.5 mL
5 oz	semi-sweet chocolate, melted and cooled	150 g
1/3 cup	all-purpose flour	75 mL
1	package (8 oz/250 g) cream cheese, softened	1
2 tbsp	unsalted butter, softened	25 mL
1/2 cup	granulated sugar	125 mL
1	egg	1
1 tbsp	all-purpose flour	15 mL
2 tbsp	sour cream	25 mL
1 tsp	vanilla	5 mL

1. CRUST: In a medium bowl, combine cookie crumbs and butter. Press into bottom and sides of pie plate and freeze.

2. FILLING: In a large mixer bowl, beat 1/3 cup (75 mL) butter and 1/3 cup (75 mL) sugar on medium-high speed for 3 minutes. Add 2 eggs, one at a time, beating after each addition. Mix in 1 1/4 tsp (6 mL) vanilla, salt and cooled chocolate. Quickly beat in 1/3 cup (75 mL) flour. Smooth into bottom of pie plate. Refrigerate for 3 minutes. In a clean mixer bowl, beat cream cheese, remaining butter and sugar on medium-high speed for 3 minutes. Add remaining egg, mixing until blended. Mix in remaining flour, sour cream and remaining vanilla. Spread batter evenly on top of brownie layer. Bake in preheated oven for 25 to 30 minutes or until the top is light brown and the center has a slight jiggle to it. Cool on a rack for 2 hours. Cover with plastic wrap and refrigerate for at least 6 hours before serving.

Turtle

CHEESE PIE

SERVES 5 TO 6

TIP
When cutting caramels, dip the knife blade in hot water to keep them from sticking to the blade.

VARIATION
Try milk chocolate instead of bittersweet for a lighter color.

Sprinkle chopped pecans over top.

Preheat oven to 325°F (160°C)
9-inch (23 cm) pie plate, ungreased

CRUST

1¼ cups	graham cracker crumbs	300 mL
3 tbsp	unsalted butter, melted	45 mL

FILLING

2	packages (each 8 oz/250 g) cream cheese, softened	2
½ cup	granulated sugar	125 mL
2	eggs	2
3 oz	bittersweet chocolate chunks	90 g
3 oz	caramels, cut into quarters	90 g
¼ cup	pecans, toasted and chopped	50 mL
½ tsp	vanilla	2 mL

DECORATION

3 oz	bittersweet chocolate	90 g

1. CRUST: In a medium bowl, combine graham cracker crumbs and butter. Press into bottom and sides of pie plate and freeze.

2. FILLING: In a large mixer bowl, beat cream cheese and sugar on medium-high speed for 3 minutes. Add eggs, one at a time, beating after each addition. Fold in chocolate chunks, caramels, pecans and vanilla. Pour batter over frozen crust. Bake in preheated oven for 25 to 35 minutes or until the top is light brown and the center has a slight jiggle to it.

3. DECORATION: While pie is still hot, grate chocolate on top of entire pie. Cool on a rack for 2 hours. Cover with plastic wrap and refrigerate for at least 6 hours before serving.

Puerto Rican Rum

CHEESE PIE

SERVES 5 TO 6

TIP
Light or clear rum is colorless and a little lighter in flavor than dark rum. Substituting dark rum in the pie will enhance the rum flavor and may make the color a bit darker.

VARIATION
Add ¼ cup (50 mL) chopped hazelnuts into the filling for flavor and crunch.

Preheat oven to 325°F (160°C)
9-inch (23 cm) pie plate, ungreased

CRUST

1¼ cups	butter cookie crumbs	300 mL
3 tbsp	unsalted butter, melted	45 mL

FILLING

2	packages (each 8 oz/250 g) cream cheese, softened	2
½ cup	packed light brown sugar	125 mL
2	eggs	2
1 tbsp	light rum	15 mL
1 tsp	ground cinnamon	5 mL
½ tsp	vanilla	2 mL

DECORATION

Classic Whipped Cream Topping (see recipe, page 172)

1. CRUST: In a medium bowl, combine butter cookie crumbs and butter. Press into bottom and sides of pie plate and freeze.

2. FILLING: In a large mixer bowl, beat cream cheese and brown sugar on medium-high speed for 3 minutes. Add eggs, one at a time, beating after each addition. Fold in rum, cinnamon and vanilla. Pour batter over frozen crust. Bake in preheated oven for 25 to 35 minutes or until the top is light brown and the center has a slight jiggle to it. Cool on a rack for 2 hours. Cover with plastic wrap and refrigerate for at least 6 hours before decorating or serving.

3. DECORATION: Ice top of pie with Classic Whipped Cream Topping or pipe rosettes around top of pie, if desired.

Citrus

CHEESE PIE

SERVES 5 TO 6

TIP
Zest the fruit the day prior to your baking and juice the fruit the day of baking. You will get more juice from your fruit.

VARIATION
Fold in ¼ cup (50 mL) fresh raspberries for a Citrus Raspberry Cheese Pie.

Preheat the oven to 325°F (160°C)
9-inch (23 cm) pie plate, ungreased

CRUST

1¼ cups	lemon cookie crumbs	300 mL
3 tbsp	unsalted butter, melted	45 mL

FILLING

2	packages (each 8 oz/250 g) cream cheese, softened	2
¾ cups	granulated sugar	175 mL
2	eggs	2
2 tbsp	lemon zest	25 mL
2 tbsp	orange zest	25 mL
1 tbsp	fresh lemon juice	15 mL
1 tbsp	fresh orange juice	15 mL
1 tsp	vanilla	5 mL

DECORATING

Classic Whipped Cream Topping (see recipe, page 172)

1. CRUST: In a bowl, combine lemon cookie crumbs and butter. Press into bottom and sides of pie plate and freeze.

2. FILLING: In a large mixer bowl, beat cream cheese and sugar on medium-high speed for 3 minutes. Add eggs, one at a time, beating after each addition. Add zests, juices and vanilla, mixing until blended. Pour batter over frozen crust. Bake in preheated oven for 25 to 35 minutes or until the top is light brown and the center has a slight jiggle to it. Cool on rack for 2 hours. Cover with plastic wrap and refrigerate for at least 6 hours before decorating or serving.

3. DECORATING: Ice the entire top with whipped cream peaks, if desired.

Savory Cheesecakes

Chipotle Chile

CHEESECAKE

SERVES 12 TO 14

TIPS

Canned chipotle chilies can be found in the international food
section of most large markets. They are smoked jalapeños with a great smoky flavor. The adobo sauce in some brands can be spicy. Use the reserved sauce to punch up chili or tomato-based sauce for spaghetti.

Preheat oven to 325°F (160°C)
6-inch (15 cm) cheesecake or springform pan with 3-inch (7.5 cm) sides, lined with parchment paper (for other pan sizes, see page 10)

CRUST

¾ cup	stone ground cracker crumbs	175 mL
2 tbsp	unsalted butter, melted	25 mL

FILLING

2	packages (each 8 oz/250 g) cream cheese, softened	2
2 tsp	granulated sugar	10 mL
1	egg	1
¼ cup	diced onions, about ⅓ of a medium-size onion	50 mL
2	cloves garlic, minced	2
2	chipotle chilies, drained and chopped	2
1	large roma tomato, seeded and diced, about ¾ cup (175 mL)	1

1. **CRUST:** In a medium bowl, combine crushed crackers and butter. Press into bottom of cheesecake pan and freeze.

2. **FILLING:** In a large mixer bowl, beat cream cheese and sugar on medium-high speed for 3 minutes. Add egg, mixing until blended. With a rubber spatula, fold in onions, garlic, chipotle chilies and tomato. Pour batter over frozen crust. Bake in preheated oven for 35 to 45 minutes or until the top is light brown and the center has a slight jiggle to it. Cool on a rack for 2 hours. Cover with plastic wrap and refrigerate for at least 6 hours before serving. Serve with crackers and/or fresh vegetables.

3. To serve as a warm appetizer, wrap the cheesecake in foil and place in a preheated 350°F (180°C) oven for 10 minutes to heat through. Do not microwave; it will toughen the cheesecake.

Creamy Crab Seafood

CHEESECAKE

Preheat oven to 325°F (160°C)

6-inch (15 cm) cheesecake or springform pan with 3-inch (7.5 cm) sides, lined with parchment paper (for other pan sizes, see page 10)

> **M**ake extra copies of this recipe before the party starts, because everyone is going to want one after they've tasted this rich cake.

SERVES 12 TO 14

TIP
Pick over the crabmeat to be sure it is free of shells.

VARIATION
Cooked lobster or scallops work well in place of the crabmeat.

FILLING

2	packages (each 8 oz/250 g) cream cheese, softened	2
8 oz	mascarpone cheese	250 g
3	eggs	3
¾ cup	all-purpose flour	175 mL
4 oz	cooked crabmeat pieces	125 g
4 oz	cooked shrimp, diced	125 g
¼ cup	diced onions, about ⅓ of a medium-size onion	50 mL
¼ cup	diced green onions, about 4 stalks	50 mL
2	cloves garlic, minced	2
½ tsp	salt	2 mL
¼ tsp	white pepper	1 mL

1. FILLING: In a large mixer bowl, beat cream cheese and mascarpone on medium-high speed for 3 minutes. Add eggs, one at a time, beating after each addition. Mix in flour. With a rubber spatula, fold in crabmeat, shrimp, onions, green onions, garlic, salt and white pepper. Pour batter into prepared cheesecake pan. Bake in preheated oven for 45 to 55 minutes or until the top is light brown and the center has a slight jiggle to it. Cool on a rack for 2 hours. Cover with plastic wrap and refrigerate for at least 6 hours before serving. Serve with crackers and/or fresh vegetables.

Maine Lobster

CHEESECAKE

SERVES 12 TO 14

TIP
People who love it hot will enjoy additional hot pepper sauce. Try 1 tbsp (15 mL) hot pepper sauce.

VARIATION
Cooked crabmeat is a delicious substitute for lobster and perhaps easier to come by.

Preheat oven to 325°F (160°C)

6-inch (15 cm) cheesecake or springform pan with 3-inch (7.5 cm) sides, lined with parchment paper (for other pan sizes, see page 10)

FILLING

2	packages (each 8 oz/250 g) cream cheese, softened	2
1 cup	sour cream	250 mL
3	eggs	3
¾ cup	all-purpose flour	175 mL
8 oz	cooked lobster pieces	250 g
¼ cup	diced onions, about ⅓ of a medium-size onion	50 mL
¼ cup	chopped green onions, about 4 stalks	50 mL
2	cloves garlic, minced	2
3	drops hot pepper sauce	3
½ tsp	salt	2 mL
¼ tsp	white pepper	1 mL

1. FILLING: In a large mixer bowl, beat cream cheese and sour cream on medium-high speed for 3 minutes. Add eggs, one at a time, beating after each addition. Mix in flour. With a rubber spatula, fold in lobster, onions, green onions, garlic, pepper sauce, salt and white pepper. Pour batter into prepared cheesecake pan. Bake in preheated oven for 45 to 55 minutes or until the top is light brown and the center has a slight jiggle to it. Cool on a rack for 2 hours. Cover with plastic wrap and refrigerate for at least 6 hours before serving. Serve with hearty crackers.

Savory Herb

CHEESECAKE

SERVES 10 TO 12

TIPS

Serve warm or cold with crackers. (See reheating instructions for Chipotle Chili Cheesecake, page 136.)

For the crust, use whatever crackers you enjoy with cheese.

VARIATION

Zest the lemon before juicing and add the zest with the fresh herbs for a wonderful aroma and extra bite of lemon.

Preheat oven to 325°F (160°C)
6-inch (15 cm) cheesecake or springform pan with 3-inch (7.5 cm) sides, lined with parchment paper (for other pan sizes, see page 10)

CRUST

¾ cup	crackers, crushed (see Tip, left)	175 mL
2 tbsp	unsalted butter, melted	25 mL

FILLING

2	packages (each 8 oz/250 g) cream cheese, softened	2
2	eggs	2
1 tsp	fresh lemon juice	5 mL
¼ tsp	salt	1 mL
1 tbsp	chopped fresh tarragon	15 mL
1½ tsp	chopped fresh thyme	7 mL
1 tsp	chopped fresh dill	5 mL
1 tsp	dried onion flakes	5 mL
½ cup	freshly grated Parmesan cheese	125 mL

1. **CRUST:** In a medium bowl, combine crackers and butter. Press into bottom of cheesecake pan and freeze.

2. **FILLING:** In a large mixer bowl, beat cream cheese on medium-high speed for 3 minutes. Add eggs, one at a time, beating after each addition. Mix in lemon juice, salt, tarragon, thyme, dill and onion flakes. With a rubber spatula, fold in Parmesan. Pour batter over frozen crust. Bake in preheated oven for 45 to 55 minutes or until the top is light brown and the center has a slight jiggle to it. Cool on a rack for 2 hours. Cover with plastic wrap and refrigerate for at least 6 hours before serving.

Blue Cheese Pistachio
CHEESECAKE 🍃

SERVES 10 TO 12

TIPS
This cheesecake can be refrigerated in the pan for up to 2 weeks before serving.

The blue cheese that is not creamed will crumble more uniformly if it is cold. The portion to be creamed should be at room temperature.

Parsley must be very dry to chop finely.

9-inch (23 cm) cheesecake or springform pan with 3-inch (7.5 cm) sides, lined with parchment paper (for other pan sizes, see page 10)

FILLING

1 cup	unsalted butter, room temperature	250 mL
1	package (8 oz/250 g) cream cheese, softened	1
1 lb	blue cheese or Gorgonzola, crumbled, divided	500 g
1	minced shallot, about ¼ cup (50 mL)	1
¼ cup	Madeira wine	50 mL
¼ tsp	white pepper	1 mL
½ cup	chopped green onion, about 8 stalks, divided	125 mL
¼ cup	chopped fresh parsley, divided	50 mL
1 cup	pistachios, toasted and chopped, divided	250 mL

DECORATION

1 cup	pistachios, toasted and chopped	250 mL

1. **FILLING:** In a food processor, fitted with a metal blade, and in two batches, if necessary, pulse butter, cream cheese and ½ lb (250 g) blue cheese, shallots, Madeira and pepper until smooth. Set aside. In prepared cheesecake pan, sprinkle half of the remaining blue cheese, half the green onions, half the parsley and ½ cup (125 mL) pistachios. Top with half the butter-cheese mixture, then layer with remaining blue cheese, green onions, parsley and pistachios. Finish with remaining butter-cheese mixture. Cover with plastic wrap and press gently to compact the layers. Chill for at least 6 hours prior to unmolding.

2. **DECORATION:** To unmold, place a large plate over top of cake and invert. Take sides of pan off, then the bottom. Peel parchment paper off cake. Pack sides with chopped pistachio nuts.

Pesto Sun-Dried Tomato
CHEESECAKE ❧

This is a great appetizer when the main course is pasta. Serve as a spread with crackers.

❧

SERVES 10 TO 12

TIP
To serve as an appetizer, place a thin slice on a lettuce leaf.

VARIATION
Substitute coarsely chopped pine nuts for grated Parmesan.

Preheat oven to 350°F (180°C)
9-inch (23 cm) cheesecake or springform pan with 3-inch (7.5 cm) sides, lined with parchment paper (for other pan sizes, see page 10)

FILLING

1 cup	tightly packed fresh basil leaves, washed and dried	250 mL
3 to 4	sprigs Italian parsley, washed and dried	3
2	cloves garlic, coarsely chopped	2
¼ cup	olive oil	50 mL
½ cup	freshly grated Parmesan cheese	125 mL
¼ tsp	salt	1 mL
¼ tsp	fresh ground pepper	1 mL
2	packages (each 8 oz/250 g) cream cheese, softened	2
2	eggs	2
¼ cup	all-purpose flour	50 mL
½ cup	chopped, drained oil-packed sun-dried tomatoes, about 10 halves	125 mL

1. FILLING: In a food processor, fitted with a metal blade, pulse basil, parsley, garlic and olive oil until finely chopped. Stir in Parmesan, salt and pepper. Set aside. In a large mixer bowl, beat cream cheese on medium-high speed for 3 minutes. Add eggs, one at a time, beating after each addition. With a rubber spatula, fold in flour. Add sun-dried tomatoes and basil mixture. Pour into prepared cheesecake pan. Bake in preheated oven for 20 to 25 minutes or until the top is light brown and the center has a slight jiggle to it. Cool on a rack for 2 hours. Cover with plastic wrap and refrigerate for at least 6 hours before serving. Serve slightly warmed, if desired, to make more spreadable. (See reheating instructions for Chipotle Chili Cheesecake, page 136.)

Swiss Alps

CHEESECAKE 🦢

Swiss cheese has a great bite to it and is such a good cooking cheese — liberate it from sandwiches!

SERVES 10 TO 12

TIPS
Serve warm or cold with crackers. (See reheating instructions for Chipotle Chili Cheesecake, page 136.)

For the crust, use your favorite salted or unsalted crackers.

VARIATION
Try Gruyère or Emmentaler cheeses for the extra rich flavor. These cheeses inspired
the generic "Swiss" style cheese.

Preheat oven to 325°F (160°C)
6-inch (23 cm) cheesecake pan, ungreased, or springform pan
with 3-inch (7.5 cm) sides, greased (for other pan sizes, see page 10)

CRUST

¾ cup	crackers, crushed (see Tip, left)	175 mL
2 tbsp	unsalted butter, melted	25 mL

FILLING

1	package (8 oz/250 g) cream cheese, softened	1
1	egg	1
1 tsp	fresh lemon juice	5 mL
¼ tsp	salt	1 mL
1 tsp	chopped fresh dill	5 mL
1 tsp	dried onion flakes	5 mL
1	clove garlic, minced	1
1 cup	shredded Swiss cheese	250 mL

1. **CRUST:** In a medium bowl, combine crackers and butter. Press into bottom of cheesecake pan and freeze.

2. **FILLING:** In a large mixer bowl, beat cream cheese on medium-high speed for 3 minutes. Add egg, mixing until blended. Add lemon juice, salt, dill, onion flakes and garlic. With a rubber spatula, fold in Swiss cheese. Pour batter over frozen crust. Bake in preheated oven for 30 to 40 minutes or until the top is light brown and the center has a slight jiggle to it. Cool on a rack for 2 hours. Cover with plastic wrap and refrigerate for at least 6 hours before serving.

Three-Cheese

TORTE

SERVES 10 TO 12

TIP

Sprinkle cracker crumbs on top for extra crunch or if the cheesecake is a little too brown on top.

VARIATION

A Swiss cheese is a good substitute for the blue cheese as its flavor blends with the other seasonings.

Preheat oven to 325°F (160°C)
6-inch (23 cm) cheesecake pan, ungreased, or springform pan with 3-inch (7.5 cm) sides, greased (for other pan sizes, see page 10)

CRUST

¾ cup	crackers, crushed (see Tip, left)	175 mL
2 tbsp	butter, melted	25 mL

FILLING

1	package (8 oz/250 g) cream cheese, softened	1
2	eggs	2
1 tsp	fresh lemon juice	5 mL
¼ tsp	salt	1 mL
1 tsp	chopped fresh dill	5 mL
1 tsp	dried onion flakes	5 mL
8 oz	blue cheese, crumbled	250 g
½ cup	freshly grated Parmesan cheese	125 mL

1. CRUST: In a medium bowl, combine crackers and butter. Press into bottom cheesecake pan and freeze.

2. FILLING: In a large mixer bowl, beat cream cheese on medium-high speed for 3 minutes. Add eggs, one at a time, beating after each addition. Stir in lemon juice, salt, dill and onion flakes. With a rubber spatula, fold in blue cheese and Parmesan. Pour batter over frozen crust. Bake in preheated oven for 30 to 40 minutes or until the top is light brown and the center has a slight jiggle to it. Cool on a rack for 2 hours. Cover with plastic wrap and refrigerate for at least 6 hours before serving.

Herbed Gorgonzola

CHEESECAKE

Preheat oven to 350°F (180°C)
9-inch (23 cm) cheesecake or springform pan with 3-inch
(7.5 cm) sides, lined with parchment paper (for other pan
sizes, see page 10)

For watching football games and other large gatherings, you need a savory cheesecake that can feed a crowd.

SERVES 18 TO 20

TIP
Serve warm or cold with crackers or party toasts. (See reheating instructions for Chipotle Chili Cheesecake, page 136.)

VARIATION
If substituting dried herbs, use half of what the recipe calls for.

CRUST

2 cups	crackers, crushed (see Tip, page 142)	500 mL
¼ cup	unsalted butter, melted	50 mL

FILLING

4	packages (each 8 oz/250 g) cream cheese, softened	4
3	eggs	3
1 tbsp	fresh lemon juice	15 mL
¼ tsp	salt	1 mL
2 tbsp	chopped fresh tarragon	25 mL
1 tsp	chopped fresh dill	5 mL
1 tsp	dried onion flakes	5 mL
8 oz	Gorgonzola cheese, crumbled	250 g

1. **CRUST:** In a medium bowl, combine cracker crumbs and butter. Press into bottom of prepared pan and freeze.

2. **FILLING:** In a large mixer bowl, beat cream cheese on medium-high speed for 3 minutes. Add eggs, one at a time, beating after each addition. Mix in lemon juice, salt, tarragon, dill and onion flakes. With a rubber spatula, fold in Gorgonzola cheese. Pour batter over frozen crust. Bake in preheated oven for 50 to 65 minutes or until the top is light brown and the center has a slight jiggle to it. Cool on a rack for 2 hours. Cover with plastic wrap and refrigerate for at least 6 hours before serving.

Holiday and Celebration Cheesecakes

Three-Tier Wedding

CHEESECAKE

Anyone who can bake a cheesecake can easily make a fabulous wedding cheesecake. Bake the cheesecakes up to three weeks in advance, freeze and defrost before decorating.

SERVES 70 TO 80

TIP
If you do not have a 6-quart (6 L) mixer, you can make this in two equal batches in a smaller stand mixer or using a hand mixer.

Preheat oven to 325°F (160°C)

8-inch (20 cm) cheesecake pan, ungreased, or springform pan with 3-inch (7.5 cm) sides, greased (for other pan sizes, see page 10)

9-inch (23 cm) cheesecake pan, ungreased, or springform pan with 3-inch (7.5 cm) sides, greased (for other pan sizes, see page 10)

10-inch (25 cm) cheesecake pan, ungreased, or springform pan with 3-inch (7.5 cm) sides, greased (for other pan sizes, see page 10)

Piping Bag

CRUST

4½ cups	graham cracker crumbs	1.125 L
¾ cup	unsalted butter, melted	175 mL

FILLING

8	packages (each 8 oz/250 g) cream cheese, softened	8
2½ cups	granulated sugar	625 mL
8	eggs	8
¼ cup	fresh lemon juice	50 mL
1 tbsp	vanilla	15 mL

TOPPING

2 cups	sour cream	500 mL
1 cup	granulated sugar	250 mL
1½ tbsp	fresh lemon juice	22 mL
2½ tsp	vanilla	12 mL

DECORATION

	Cream Cheese Whipped Cream (see recipe, right)	
12 cups	fresh strawberries, cleaned and green tops sliced off	3 L

1. CRUST: In a medium bowl, mix graham cracker crumbs and butter. Press 2 cups (500 mL) into 10-inch (25 cm) cheesecake pan, press 1½ cups (375 mL) into 9-inch (23 cm) cheesecake pan and press 1 cup (250 mL) into 8-inch (20 cm) cheesecake pan. Place in freezer.

TIP
Do not substitute
flavored whipped
cream for the Cream
Cheese Whipped
Cream recipe. The
cream cheese recipe
will hold the form
of piped borders
and decorations
much longer.

VARIATION
Use an array of fresh
berries, such as
raspberries, blueber-
ries, blackberries.
Also
use fresh flowers,
such as roses, but
make sure they have
not been sprayed
with pesticides.

2. FILLING: In a large mixer bowl, in two batches, if necessary, beat cream cheese and sugar on medium-high speed for 5 to 6 minutes. Add eggs, one at a time, beating after each addition. Mix in lemon juice and vanilla. Pour half the batter into 10-inch (25 cm) frozen cheesecake bottom. Pour about three-quarters remaining batter into 9-inch (23 cm) cheesecake bottom. Pour remaining batter into 8-inch (20 cm) cheesecake bottom. Check to make sure depth of batter is approximately the same in each pan. Bake in preheated oven or until the tops are light brown and the centers have a slight jiggle. The large cheesecake will take about 75 to 80 minutes to bake; the medium will take about 45 to 55 minutes; and the small will take about 35 to 40 minutes. Cool on the counter for 10 minutes (do not turn the oven off). The cakes will sink slightly. All three may not fit on one center rack, so bake in two batches, if necessary.

3. TOPPING: In a medium bowl, combine sour cream, sugar, lemon juice and vanilla. Divide mixture in same proportions as batter and pour into center of each of the cooled cakes and spread out to edges. Bake for 5 minutes more. Cool on a rack for 2 hours. Cover and refrigerate for at least 8 hours before decorating, or freeze up to 3 weeks before decorating. (See Storing and Freezing, page 19).

4. DECORATION: Prepare the Cream Cheese Whipped Cream (see recipe, below). Using a star tip, pipe in a rope fashion around the border of each cake. Top each cake with whole strawberries, cut side down. Do not attempt to stack cakes one on top of the other. Instead, place cakes on a three-tiered pedestal cake plate or on three different plates at different heights.

5. CREAM CHEESE WHIPPED CREAM: In a mixer bowl with whip attachment, whip 3 oz (90 g) softened cream cheese with 1 tbsp (15 mL) milk on low speed until smooth, about 3 minutes. Pour in 2 cups (500 mL) whipping (35%) cream and ¾ cup (175 mL) confectioner's (icing) sugar. Whip on high speed, scraping bowl occasionally, until stiff peaks form. Makes about 2½ cups (625 mL).

4th of July

CHEESECAKE

SERVES 18 TO 20

TIP
You can make the cheesecake weeks ahead and freeze it. Decorate the day of the event.

VARIATION
Substitute fresh cherries for the strawberries to keep the patriotic theme. Using all of one berry is delicious, but not as colorful.

Preheat oven to 350°F (180°C)
10-inch (25 cm) cheesecake pan, ungreased, or springform pan with 3-inch (7.5 cm) sides, greased (for other pan sizes, see page 10)

CRUST

2 cups	butter cookie crumbs	500 mL
1/3 cup	unsalted butter, melted	75 mL

FILLING

6	packages (each 8 oz/250 g) cream cheese, softened	6
2 1/4 cups	granulated sugar	550 mL
6	eggs	6
1 cup	fresh strawberries, cut into quarters	250 mL
1/2 cup	fresh raspberries	125 mL
1/2 cup	fresh blueberries	125 mL
1 tbsp	vanilla	15 mL

DECORATION

1/2 cup	whipping (35%) cream	125 mL
2 tbsp	granulated sugar	25 mL
1 cup	fresh strawberries, with tops cut off	250 mL
1/2 cup	fresh raspberries	125 mL
1/2 cup	fresh blueberries	125 mL

1. CRUST: In a medium bowl, combine cookie crumbs and butter. Press into bottom of cheesecake pan and freeze.

2. FILLING: In a large mixer bowl, beat cream cheese and sugar on medium-high speed for 5 minutes. Add eggs, one at a time, beating after each addition. Fold in strawberries, raspberries, blueberries and vanilla. Pour batter over frozen crust. Bake in preheated oven for 60 to 75 minutes or until the top is light brown and the center has a slight jiggle to it. Cool on a rack for 2 hours. Cover with plastic wrap and refrigerate for at least 8 hours before decorating or serving.

3. DECORATION: In a well-chilled bowl, whip cream on medium-high speed until soft peaks form. With the mixer still running, sprinkle sugar into cream and continue whipping until firm peaks form. Top entire cake with whipped cream. Place perfectly shaped strawberries around outside edge of cake, followed by a row of raspberries. Fill in the center with blueberries.

Autumn Festival

CHEESECAKE

F*ull of warm harvest flavors, this cheesecake is great served on a cool autumn night or Halloween.*

SERVES 18 TO 20

TIP
If the raisins are hard, you can plump them up in a little hot water. Cover them for 10 minutes, then drain and use.

Preheat oven to 350°F (180°C)
10-inch (25 cm) cheesecake pan, ungreased, or springform pan
with 3-inch (7.5 cm) sides, greased (for other pan sizes, see page 10)

CRUST

1 1/2 cups	graham cracker crumbs	375 mL
1/2 cup	pecans, toasted and ground	125 mL
1/3 cup	unsalted butter, melted	75 mL

FILLING

6	packages (each 8 oz/250 g) cream cheese, softened	6
2 1/4 cups	granulated sugar	550 mL
6	eggs	6
1	medium baking apple, peeled and chopped fine	1
1/2 cup	golden raisins	125 mL
2 tbsp	orange zest	25 mL
1 tsp	each ground nutmeg and cinnamon	5 mL
1/2 tsp	each ground cloves and allspice	2 mL
2 tsp	vanilla	10 mL

DECORATION

1/2 cup	whipping (35%) cream	125 mL
2 tbsp	granulated sugar	25 mL
1/4 tsp	orange zest	1 mL
1 tsp	ground cinnamon	5 mL
1/2 tsp	ground nutmeg	2 mL

1. **CRUST:** In a bowl, combine graham cracker crumbs, pecans and butter. Press into pan and freeze.

2. **FILLING:** In a large bowl, beat cream cheese and sugar on medium-high speed for 5 minutes. Add eggs, one at a time, beating after each addition. Fold in chopped apple, raisins, orange zest, nutmeg, cinnamon, cloves, allspice and vanilla. Pour over frozen crust. Bake for 60 to 75 minutes or until the top is light brown. Cool for 2 hours. Cover and refrigerate for 8 hours before decorating or serving.

3. **DECORATION:** Whip cream on medium-high until soft peaks form. With the mixer still running, sprinkle in sugar and continue whipping until firm peaks form. Fold in zest, cinnamon and nutmeg. Spread on cake.

Birthday Chocolate

CHEESECAKE

Here's a happy birthday recipe to satisfy all the chocolate lovers in your family.

SERVES 18 TO 20

TIP
Make chocolate shavings with a potato peeler on a cold chocolate bar or by moving a spatula in an up and down motion on the side of a large chocolate bar.

VARIATION
Add 1 cup (250 mL) semi-sweet chocolate chips that have been dusted with 1 tbsp (15 mL) flour into the batter for a chocolate chocolate-chip cheesecake.

Preheat oven to 350°F (180°C)
10-inch (25 cm) cheesecake pan, ungreased, or springform pan with 3-inch (7.5 cm) sides, greased (for other pan sizes, see page 10)

CRUST

2½ cups	chocolate sandwich cookie crumbs	625 mL
⅓ cup	unsalted butter, melted	75 mL

FILLING

6	packages (each 8 oz/250 g) cream cheese, softened	6
2 cups	granulated sugar	500 mL
6	eggs	6
½ cup	unsweetened cocoa powder, sifted	125 mL
2 tbsp	all-purpose flour	25 mL
1 cup	sour cream	250 mL
2 tsp	vanilla	10 mL

DECORATION

	Classic Whipping Cream Topping (see recipe, page 172)	
3 oz	semi-sweet chocolate, shaved	90 g

1. CRUST: In a medium bowl, combine cookie crumbs and butter. Press into bottom of cheesecake pan and freeze.

2. FILLING: In a large mixer bowl, beat cream cheese and sugar on medium-high speed for 5 minutes. Add eggs, one at a time, beating after each addition. Beat in cocoa powder and flour. Mix in sour cream and vanilla. Pour batter over frozen crust. Bake in preheated oven for 75 to 85 minutes or until the top is light brown and the center has a slight jiggle to it. Cool on a rack for 2 hours. Cover with plastic wrap and refrigerate for at least 8 hours before decorating or serving.

3. DECORATION: Ice top of cake with Classic Whipped Cream Topping or pipe rosettes around top of cake, if desired. Top each with chocolate shavings (see Tip, left).

Easter

CHEESECAKE ❧

E*aster always reminds me of white chocolate and toasted coconut. This cheesecake will be a hit at Easter brunch or any spring party.* ❧

SERVES 18 TO 20

TIP
Make sure the chocolate has cooled slightly or the cake will have chocolate chunks in the batter.

VARIATION
Pecans may be more economical than macadamia nuts.

Preheat oven to 350°F (180°C)
10-inch (25 cm) cheesecake pan, ungreased, or springform pan with 3-inch (7.5 cm) sides, greased (for other pan sizes, see page 10)

CRUST

2 cups	butter cookie crumbs	500 mL
½ cup	ground macadamia nuts	125 mL
¼ cup	unsalted butter, melted	50 mL

FILLING

6	packages (each 8 oz/250 g) cream cheese, softened	6
2 cups	granulated sugar	500 mL
5	eggs	5
1	egg yolk	1
2 tsp	vanilla	10 mL
8 oz	white chocolate, melted and cooled	250 g
1½ cups	flaked coconut, toasted (see Tip, page 59)	375 mL

DECORATION

	Classic Whipped Cream Topping (see recipe, page 172)	
½ cup	flaked coconut, toasted	125 mL

1. CRUST: In a medium bowl, combine cookie crumbs, macadamia nuts and butter. Press into bottom of cheesecake pan and freeze.

2. FILLING: In a large mixer bowl, beat cream cheese and sugar on medium-high speed for 5 minutes. Add eggs and egg yolk, one at a time, beating after each addition. Mix in vanilla and melted chocolate. Fold in coconut. Pour batter over frozen crust. Bake in preheated oven for 60 to 75 minutes or until the top is light brown and the center has a slight jiggle to it. Cool on a rack for 2 hours. Cover with plastic wrap and refrigerate for at least 8 hours before decorating or serving.

3. DECORATION: Ice top of cake with Classic Whipped Cream Topping or pipe a border around edge of cake, if desired. Sprinkle with toasted coconut.

Passover Honey

CHEESECAKE

SERVES 18 TO 20

TIPS
Grind nuts and matzo meal together in a food processor to keep the nuts from turning to butter.

Save the egg whites in the refrigerator for 2 days or the freezer for up to 6 months. Use for meringue or when a recipe calls for egg whites.

VARIATION
Substitute pecans for almonds for a more complex nut flavor.

Preheat oven to 350°F (180°C)
10-inch (25 cm) cheesecake pan, ungreased, or springform pan with 3-inch (7.5 cm) sides, greased (for other pan sizes, see page 10)

CRUST

2 cups	ground almonds	500 mL
¼ cup	matzo meal, ground	50 mL
2 tbsp	unsalted butter, melted	25 mL

FILLING

4	packages (each 8 oz/250 g) cream cheese, softened	4
2 cups	sour cream	500 mL
⅔ cup	liquid honey	150 mL
6	egg yolks	6
1 tbsp	vanilla	15 mL
½ cup	ground almonds	125 mL

1. CRUST: In a medium bowl, combine almonds, matzo meal and butter. Press into bottom of cheesecake pan and freeze.

2. FILLING: In a large mixer bowl, beat cream cheese, sour cream and honey on medium-high speed for 3 minutes. Add egg yolks, one at a time, beating after each addition. Fold in vanilla. Pour batter over frozen crust. Sprinkle chopped almonds on top of batter. Bake for 60 to 75 minutes or until the top is light brown and the center has a slight jiggle to it. Cool on a rack for 2 hours. Cover with plastic wrap and refrigerate for at least 6 hours before decorating or serving.

Maple Pumpkin

CHEESECAKE ❧

> T wo flavors for the fall that go well together are maple and pumpkin. ❧

SERVES 18 TO 20

TIP
If maple syrup is not available you can use about ¼ tsp (1 mL) pure maple flavoring.

VARIATION
Add 1 cup (250 mL) chopped hazelnuts into the batter for a crunchy texture.

Preheat oven to 350°F (180°C)
10-inch (25 cm) cheesecake pan, ungreased, or springform pan with 3-inch (7.5 cm) sides, greased (for other pan sizes, see page 10)

CRUST

2½ cups	graham cracker crumbs	375 mL
1 tsp	ground ginger	5 mL
⅓ cup	unsalted butter, melted	75 mL

FILLING

5	packages (each 8 oz/250 g) cream cheese, softened	5
1 cup	sour cream	250 mL
2¼ cups	granulated sugar	550 mL
6	eggs	6
½ cup	all-purpose flour	125 mL
1 cup	pumpkin purée (not pie filling)	250 mL
1 tbsp	vanilla	15 mL
3 tbsp	fresh lemon juice	45 mL
½ cup	pure maple syrup	125 mL
1 tbsp	ground cinnamon	15 mL
½ tsp	ground nutmeg	2 mL
¼ tsp	ground allspice	1 mL

DECORATION

Classic Whipped Cream Topping
(see recipe, page 172)

1. CRUST: In a medium bowl, combine graham cracker crumbs, ginger and butter. Press into bottom of cheesecake pan and freeze.

2. FILLING: In a large mixer bowl, beat cream cheese, sour cream and sugar on medium-high speed for 5 minutes. Add eggs, one at a time, beating after each addition. Mix in flour, pumpkin, vanilla, lemon juice, maple syrup, cinnamon, nutmeg and allspice. Pour batter over frozen crust. Bake in preheated oven for 65 to 75 minutes or until the top is light brown and the center has a slight jiggle to it. Cool on a rack for 2 hours. Cover with plastic wrap and refrigerate for at least 8 hours before decorating or serving.

3. DECORATION: Ice top of cake with Classic Whipped Cream Topping or pipe a border around edge of cake, if desired.

Pumpkin Praline

CHEESECAKE

SERVES 18 TO 20

TIP
Look for pure pumpkin when purchasing canned pumpkin. Stay clear of the pumpkin pie filling and those with squash added.

VARIATION
Hazelnuts work well instead of pecans in this recipe also.

Preheat oven to 350°F (180°C)
10-inch (25 cm) cheesecake pan, ungreased, or springform pan
with 3-inch (7.5 cm) sides, greased (for other pan sizes, see page 10)

CRUST

2 1/2 cups	gingersnap cookie crumbs	625 mL
1/3 cup	unsalted butter, melted	75 mL

FILLING

5	packages (each 8 oz/250 g) cream cheese, softened	5
1 cup	sour cream	250 mL
2 1/4 cups	granulated sugar	550 mL
6	eggs	6
1/2 cup	all-purpose flour	125 mL
1 cup	pumpkin purée (not pie filling)	250 mL
1 tbsp	vanilla	15 mL
2 tsp	ground cinnamon	10 mL
1/2 tsp	ground nutmeg	2 mL
1/4 tsp	each ground allspice and cloves	1 mL
1 cup	pecans, toasted and chopped	250 mL

DECORATION

	Classic Whipped Cream Topping (see recipe, page 172)	
1 tsp	ground cinnamon	5 mL
18 to 20	pecan halves	18 to 20

1. **CRUST:** In a medium bowl, combine cookie crumbs and butter. Press into bottom of cheesecake pan and freeze.

2. **FILLING:** In a large mixer bowl, beat cream cheese, sour cream and sugar on medium-high speed for 5 minutes. Add eggs, one at a time, beating after each addition. Mix in flour, pumpkin, vanilla, cinnamon, nutmeg, allspice, cloves and pecans. Pour batter over frozen crust. Bake in preheated oven for 65 to 75 minutes or until the top is light brown and the center has a slight jiggle to it. Cool on a rack for 2 hours. Cover with plastic wrap and refrigerate for at least 8 hours before decorating or serving.

3. **DECORATING:** Ice top of cake with Classic Whipped Cream Topping or pipe a border around edge of cake, if desired. Sprinkle with cinnamon and pecan halves.

Sweet Potato

CHEESECAKE

SERVES 18 TO 20

TIP
Peel the potato,
wrap in foil and bake
for 60 minutes in a
400°F (200°C) oven or
until soft. Use canned
sweet potatoes, if
fresh are unavailable.

Preheat oven to 350°F (180°C)
10-inch (25 cm) cheesecake pan, ungreased, or springform pan
with 3-inch (7.5 cm) sides, greased (for other pan sizes, see page 10)

CRUST

2 cups	pecans, ground	500 mL
¼ cup	all-purpose flour	50 mL
2 tbsp	unsalted butter, melted	25 mL

FILLING

5	packages (each 8 oz/250 g) cream cheese, softened	5
1 cup	sour cream	250 mL
2 cups	packed light brown sugar	500 mL
6	egg yolks	6
1 tbsp	vanilla	15 mL
1½ tsp	ground nutmeg	7 mL
6	egg whites	6
4 oz	sweet potato, cooked and mashed, about half medium-size sweet potato (see Tip, left)	125 g

DECORATION

	Classic Whipped Cream Topping (see recipe, page 172)	
1 tsp	ground nutmeg	5 mL

1. CRUST: In a medium bowl, combine pecans, flour and butter. Press into bottom of cheesecake pan and freeze.

2. FILLING: In a large mixer bowl, beat cream cheese, sour cream and brown sugar on medium-high speed for 5 minutes. Add egg yolks, one at a time, beating after each addition. Fold in vanilla and nutmeg. In a clean bowl, whip egg whites until soft peaks form. Fold in sweet potatoes. Fold into batter. Pour batter over frozen crust. Bake in preheated oven for 60 to 75 minutes or until the top is light brown and the center has a slight jiggle to it. Cool on a rack for 2 hours. Cover and refrigerate for 8 hours before decorating or serving.

3. DECORATION: Top entire cake with whipped cream or pipe rosettes around border, if desired. Sprinkle with fresh ground nutmeg.

Christmas

CHEESECAKE

Preheat oven to 350°F (180°C)
10-inch (25 cm) cheesecake pan, ungreased, or springform pan
with 3-inch (7.5 cm) sides, greased (for other pan sizes, see page 10)

G*ive in to the Christmas spirit of red and green everything by garnishing this cheesecake with raspberry preserves and a ring of sliced kiwi.*

SERVES 18 TO 20

TIPS
When choosing kiwis they should be firm like tomatoes with a little give when you hold
one in the palm of your hand.

Preserves are best to use here rather than jellies or jams. They adhere to the cheesecake better because they are thicker and less runny.

VARIATION
Substitute strawberry preserves for the raspberry preserves.

CRUST

2 cups	graham cracker crumbs	500 mL
¼ cup	pecans, coarsely ground	50 mL
⅓ cup	unsalted butter, melted	75 mL

FILLING

5	packages (each 8 oz/250 g) cream cheese, softened	5
2¼ cups	granulated sugar	550 mL
1 cup	sour cream	250 mL
6	eggs	6
⅓ cup	all-purpose flour	75 mL
1 tbsp	orange zest	15 mL
1 tbsp	lemon zest	15 mL
1 tsp	fresh lemon juice	5 mL
2 tsp	vanilla	10 mL

DECORATION

½ cup	whipping (35%) cream	125 mL
2 tbsp	granulated sugar	25 mL
⅔ cup	raspberry preserves	150 mL
2	kiwis, peeled and sliced thin	2

1. CRUST: In a bowl, combine graham cracker crumbs, pecans and butter. Press into cheesecake pan and freeze.

2. FILLING: In a large mixer bowl, beat cream cheese, sugar and sour cream on medium-high speed for 5 minutes. Add eggs, one at a time, beating after each addition. Mix in flour, zests, juice and vanilla. Pour batter over frozen crust. Bake in preheated oven for 60 to 75 minutes or until the top is light brown and the center has a slight jiggle to it. Cool on a rack for 2 hours. Cover with plastic wrap and refrigerate for at least 8 hours before decorating or serving.

3. DECORATION: In a well-chilled bowl, whip cream on medium-high speed until soft peaks form. With the mixer still running, sprinkle sugar into cream and continue whipping until firm peaks form. Pipe a border around edge of cooled cake. Spread raspberry preserves into the center and outward towards the whipped cream. Lay kiwi slices in spirals close to the whipped cream.

Cranberry Orange

CHEESECAKE

SERVES 18 TO 20

TIP
Use frozen cranberries right from the freezer without thawing to prevent the color from bleeding.

VARIATION
Spread top with Spiked Cranberry Sauce (see recipe, page 184).

Preheat oven to 350°F (180°C)
10-inch (25 cm) cheesecake pan, ungreased, or springform pan with 3-inch (7.5 cm) sides, greased (for other pan sizes, see page 10)

CRUST

1½ cups	butter cookie crumbs	375 mL
½ cup	pecans, toasted and ground	125 mL
⅓ cup	unsalted butter, melted	75 mL

FILLING

6	packages (each 8 oz/250 g) cream cheese, softened	6
2¼ cups	granulated sugar	550 mL
6	eggs	6
2 tbsp	orange zest	25 mL
2 tsp	ground nutmeg	10 mL
2 tsp	vanilla	10 mL
1½ cups	fresh cranberries, crushed slightly, or frozen cranberries	375 mL

TOPPING

1 cup	sour cream	250 mL
½ cup	granulated sugar	125 mL
1 tsp	vanilla	5 mL
¼ tsp	orange zest	1 mL

1. CRUST: In a medium bowl, combine cookie crumbs, pecans and butter. Press into bottom of cheesecake pan and freeze.

2. FILLING: In a large mixer bowl, beat cream cheese and sugar on medium-high speed for 5 minutes. Add eggs, one at a time, beating after each addition. Fold in orange zest, nutmeg and vanilla. Fold in cranberries. Pour over frozen crust. Bake in preheated oven for 60 to 75 minutes or until the top is light brown and the center has a slight jiggle to it. Cool on the counter for 10 minutes (do not turn the oven off). The cake will sink slightly.

3. TOPPING: In a small bowl, combine sour cream, sugar, vanilla and zest. Pour mixture into center of cooled cake and spread out to edges. Bake for 5 minutes more. Cool on a rack for 2 hours. Cover and refrigerate for at least 8 hours before serving.

Eggnog Nutmeg Rum

CHEESECAKE

SERVES 18 TO 20

TIP
Keep canned eggnog in the pantry for making this recipe out of season when you can't wait for fresh cartons of eggnog to be available.

Preheat oven to 350°F (180°C)
10-inch (25 cm) cheesecake pan, ungreased, or springform pan with 3-inch (7.5 cm) sides, greased (for other pan sizes, see page 10)

CRUST

2 cups	graham cracker crumbs	500 mL
1 tsp	ground nutmeg	5 mL
1/3 cup	unsalted butter, melted	75 mL

FILLING

4	packages (each 8 oz/250 g) cream cheese, softened	4
2 cups	small curd cottage cheese, drained (see Tip, page 36)	500 mL
2 1/4 cups	granulated sugar	550 mL
6	eggs	6
1 cup	prepared eggnog	250 mL
1/2 cup	light rum	125 mL
1 tbsp	vanilla	15 mL
1 tsp	ground nutmeg	5 mL

TOPPING

1 cup	sour cream	250 mL
1/2 cup	granulated sugar	125 mL
1 tsp	vanilla	5 mL
1 tsp	ground nutmeg	5 mL

DECORATION

1/2 cup	whipping (35%) cream	125 mL
2 tbsp	granulated sugar	25 mL
1 tsp	ground nutmeg	5 mL

VARIATION
Substitute cinnamon
for nutmeg or use in
addition to nutmeg
for extra sparkle in
the decorating.

1. CRUST: In a medium bowl, combine graham cracker crumbs, nutmeg and butter. Press into bottom of cheese-cake pan and freeze.

2. FILLING: In a large mixer bowl, beat cream cheese, cottage cheese and sugar on medium-high speed for 5 minutes. Add eggs, one at a time, beating after each addition. Fold in eggnog, rum, vanilla and nutmeg. Pour over frozen crust. Bake in preheated oven for 60 to 75 minutes or until the top is light brown and the center has a slight jiggle to it. Cool on the counter for 10 minutes (do not turn the oven off). The cake will sink slightly.

3. TOPPING: In a small bowl, combine sour cream, sugar, vanilla and nutmeg. Pour mixture into center of cooled cake and spread out to edges. Bake for 5 minutes more. Cool on a rack for 2 hours. Cover and refrigerate for at least 8 hours before decorating or serving.

4. DECORATION: In a well-chilled bowl, whip cream on medium-high speed until soft peaks form. With the mixer still running, sprinkle sugar into cream and continue whipping until firm peaks form. Ice top of cake with whipped cream or pipe rosettes around top of cake, if desired. Sprinkle with nutmeg.

Peppermint Chocolate

CHEESECAKE

SERVES 18 TO 20

TIP
Cool the chocolate before mixing with the cold batter or you will end up with a chocolate chip cake instead.

VARIATION
Use white chocolate chunks instead of the semi-sweet chocolate.

Preheat oven to 350°F (180°C)
10-inch (25 cm) cheesecake pan, ungreased, or springform pan with 3-inch (7.5 cm) sides, greased (for other pan sizes, see page 10)

CRUST

2 cups	chocolate sandwich cookie crumbs	500 mL
1/3 cup	unsalted butter, melted	75 mL

FILLING

6	packages (each 8 oz/250 g) cream cheese, softened	6
2 cups	granulated sugar	500 mL
6	eggs	6
1/2 cup	all-purpose flour	125 mL
1 cup	sour cream	250 mL
2 tsp	vanilla	10 mL
1/2 tsp	peppermint extract	2 mL
6 oz	semi-sweet chocolate, melted and cooled	175 g
12 oz	semi-sweet chocolate chunks	375 g
1 cup	crushed candy canes	250 mL
2 tbsp	all-purpose flour	25 mL

DECORATION

	Classic Whipped Cream Topping (see recipe, page 172)	
1/4 cup	crushed candy canes	50 mL

1. CRUST: In a medium bowl, combine cookie crumbs and butter. Press into bottom of cheesecake pan and freeze.

2. FILLING: In a large bowl, beat cream cheese and sugar on medium-high for 5 minutes. Add eggs, one at a time, beating after each addition. Mix in flour, sour cream, vanilla, peppermint extract and melted chocolate. In a small bowl, coat chocolate chunks and candy canes with flour. Fold into batter. Pour over frozen crust. Bake in preheated oven for 60 to 75 minutes or until the top is light brown. Cool for 2 hours. Cover and refrigerate for 8 hours before decorating.

3. DECORATION: Ice top of cake with Classic Whipped Cream Topping or pipe a border around edge of cake, if desired. Top with crushed candy canes.

Guilt-Free Cheesecakes

Tropical Cheesecake (page 170)

Almond

CHEESECAKE

Preheat oven to 325°F (160°C)
9-inch (23 cm) cheesecake pan, ungreased, or springform pan
with 3-inch (7.5 cm) sides, greased (for other pan sizes, see page 10)

> The almonds create such a rich flavor you won't believe this is a lower-calorie cheesecake.

SERVES 10 TO 12

TIP
Although nuts are high in calories, a little bit adds a lot of flavor.

VARIATION
Spike the almond flavor with 2 tbsp (25 mL) almond liqueur.

CRUST

1½ cups	almond cookie crumbs	375 mL
3 tbsp	margarine, melted	45 mL

FILLING

2	packages (each 8 oz/250 g) Neufchâtel cheese or light cream cheese, softened	2
1 cup	lower-fat sour cream	250 mL
1 cup	granulated sugar	250 mL
3	eggs	3
3 tbsp	all-purpose flour	45 mL
¼ cup	almonds, toasted and chopped	50 mL
1 tsp	vanilla	5 mL
¼ tsp	ground allspice	1 mL

DECORATION

8 oz	lower-fat whipped topping	250 g
¼ cup	ground almonds	50 mL

1. CRUST: In a medium bowl, combine almond cookie crumbs and margarine. Press into bottom of cheesecake pan and freeze.

2. FILLING: In a large mixer bowl, beat cheese, sour cream and sugar on medium-high speed for 3 minutes. Add eggs, one at a time, beating after each addition. Fold in flour, almonds, vanilla and allspice. Pour over frozen crust. Bake for 45 to 55 minutes or until the top is light brown and the center has a slight jiggle to it. Cool on a rack for 2 hours. Cover with plastic wrap and refrigerate for at least 6 hours before decorating.

3. DECORATING: Top with whipped topping and dust with a sprinkling of ground almonds.

Light Espresso

CHESECAKE

Two shots
of high-octane
espresso create
a creamy café au
lait dessert.

SERVES 10 TO 12

TIP
You can use two
shots of espresso in
the topping instead
of the powder and
water.

Preheat oven to 325°F (160°C)
9-inch (23 cm) cheesecake pan, ungreased, or springform pan
with 3-inch (7.5 cm) sides, greased (for other pan sizes, see page 10)

CRUST

1½ cups	chocolate sandwich cookie crumbs	375 mL
3 tbsp	margarine, melted	45 mL

FILLING

2	packages (each 8 oz/250 g) Neufchâtel cheese or light cream cheese, softened	2
¾ cup	granulated sugar	175 mL
2	eggs	2
2 tbsp	all-purpose flour	25 mL
1 tbsp	instant espresso powder	15 mL
1 tbsp	hot water	15 mL
1 tsp	vanilla	5 mL

DECORATION

¼ cup	instant espresso powder	50 mL
2 tsp	hot water	10 mL
8 oz	lower-fat whipped topping	250 g

1. CRUST: In a medium bowl, combine cookie crumbs and margarine. Press into bottom of cheesecake pan and freeze.

2. FILLING: In a large mixer bowl, beat cheese and sugar on medium-high speed for 3 minutes. Add eggs, one at a time, beating after each addition. Mix in flour. In a small bowl, dissolve espresso powder in hot water. Mix dissolved espresso and vanilla into batter. Pour batter over frozen crust. Bake in preheated oven for 35 to 45 minutes or until the top is light brown and the center has a slight jiggle to it. Cool on a rack for 2 hours. Cover with plastic wrap and refrigerate for at least 6 hours before decorating or serving.

3. DECORATION: In a medium bowl, dissolve espresso powder in hot water. Beat espresso mixture into whipped topping. Spread evenly over cake.

Fresh Berry

CHEESECAKE 🦢

SERVES 10 TO 12

TIP
Cut the strawberries in smaller pieces to avoid pockets of liquid in the cheesecake.

VARIATION
Use all one kind of berry or just blueberries, if desired.

Preheat oven to 325°F (160°C)
9-inch (23 cm) cheesecake pan, ungreased, or springform pan with 3-inch (7.5 cm) sides, greased (for other pan sizes, see page 10)

CRUST

1½ cups	butter cookie crumbs	375 mL
3 tbsp	margarine, melted	45 mL

FILLING

4	packages (each 8 oz/250 g) Neufchâtel cheese or light cream cheese, softened	4
1 cup	granulated sugar	250 mL
4	eggs	4
¼ cup	all-purpose flour	50 mL
1 cup	fresh strawberries, chopped	250 mL
½ cup	fresh raspberries	125 mL
1 tsp	vanilla	5 mL

DECORATION

8 oz	lower-fat whipped topping	250 g
¼ cup	fresh strawberries	50 mL
¼ cup	fresh raspberries	50 mL

1. CRUST: In a medium bowl, combine butter cookie crumbs and margarine. Press into bottom of cheesecake pan and freeze.

2. FILLING: In a large mixer bowl, beat cheese and sugar on medium-high speed for 3 minutes. Add eggs, one at a time, beating after each addition. Mix in flour. Fold in strawberries, raspberries and vanilla. Pour over frozen crust. Bake in preheated oven for 45 to 55 minutes or until the top is light brown and the center has a slight jiggle to it. Cool on a rack for 2 hours. Cover with plastic wrap and refrigerate for at least 6 hours before decorating or serving.

3. DECORATION: Spread whipped topping evenly over cake. Decorate with fresh berries.

Berry Cheesecake

PARFAIT

SERVES 8

TIP
These only keep for about 2 days before getting a rubbery texture.

To make a sugar-free version, substitute the equivalent amount of a granular sugar substitute such as sucralose. This type of sweetener is stable when cooked.

VARIATION
Swirl the berries into the batter.

Eight 3-inch (7.5 cm) stemmed glasses

FILLING

2	packets (each ¼ oz/7.5 g) powdered unflavored gelatin	2
½ cup	milk	125 mL
⅔ cup	granulated sugar	150 mL
2	eggs	2
¼ cup	fresh lemon juice	50 mL
2 lbs	lower-fat cottage cheese	1 kg
1 tbsp	vanilla	15 mL

DECORATION

1 cup	fresh berries	250 mL

1. FILLING: In a small saucepan, sprinkle gelatin over milk and let stand for 1 minute. Place over low heat and stir until gelatin is completely dissolved. Set aside to cool slightly.

2. In a heatproof bowl or top of double boiler, whisk sugar and eggs until blended. Whisk in lemon juice. Place over simmering water and cook, whisking constantly, for about 5 minutes, until light and thickened. Set aside to cool slightly.

3. In a food processor, fitted with a metal blade, purée cottage cheese and vanilla until very smooth, about 3 minutes. Scrape down sides of bowl and process another 2 minutes. Add gelatin and egg mixtures and process until blended. Pour immediately into eight glasses. Place in refrigerator until set.

4. DECORATION: When set, garnish each glass with a few berries.

Joy's
CHEESECAKE CUPS

SERVES 8

TIP
Swirl the preserves
into the batter before
baking for a rich look.

VARIATION
Use whole raspberries
or strawberries to
garnish instead
of preserves.

Preheat oven to 300°F (150°C)
Eight 3-inch (7.5 cm) custard cups, sprayed with nonstick spray
Large baking pan with 2-inch (5 cm) sides

FILLING

3 cups	lower-fat cottage cheese	750 mL
1 tbsp	vanilla	15 mL
12	packets artificial sweetener	12
2	eggs	2

DECORATION

½ cup	raspberry preserves	125 mL

1. FILLING: In a food processor, fitted with a metal blade, combine cottage cheese, vanilla, artificial sweetener and eggs until very smooth, about 3 minutes. Scrape down sides of bowl and process another 2 minutes. Spoon into custard cups. Put cups into baking pan filled with enough boiling water to come halfway up the cups. Bake for 20 to 25 minutes or until centers are no longer loose when moved. Cool on a rack for 30 minutes. Cover and refrigerate for at least 2 hours before decorating.

2. DECORATION: Garnish each custard cup with 1 tbsp (15 mL) raspberry preserves.

Fresh Tangerine

CHEESECAKE ❧

Using fresh fruit makes all the difference in the taste and texture of this cheesecake.

❧

SERVES 10 TO 12

TIP
You can use tangerine zest in other recipes in place of orange zest.

VARIATION
Add tangerine zest to the crust for a boost of citrus flavor.

Preheat oven to 325°F (160°C)
9-inch (23 cm) cheesecake pan, ungreased, or springform pan with 3-inch (7.5 cm) sides, greased (for other pan sizes, see page 10)

CRUST

1½ cups	butter cookie crumbs	375 mL
3 tbsp	margarine, melted	45 mL

FILLING

2	packages (each 8 oz/250 g) Neufchâtel cheese or light cream cheese, softened	2
1 cup	lower-fat sour cream	250 mL
8 oz	lower-fat cottage cheese, puréed	250 g
1 cup	granulated sugar	250 mL
4	eggs	4
¼ cup	all-purpose flour	50 mL
1 tbsp	fresh lemon juice	15 mL
1 tbsp	orange juice concentrate	15 mL
1 tsp	tangerine zest	5 mL
1 tsp	vanilla	5 mL
1	medium tangerine, diced, about ½ cup (125 mL)	1

DECORATION

8 oz	lower-fat whipped topping	250 g
1	medium tangerine, cut into 12 segments	1

1. CRUST: In a medium bowl, combine cookie crumbs and margarine. Press into bottom of cheesecake pan and freeze.

2. FILLING: In a large mixer bowl, beat cheese, sour cream, cottage cheese and sugar on medium-high speed for 3 minutes. Add eggs, one at a time, beating after each addition. Fold in flour, lemon juice, orange juice, zest and vanilla. Fold in tangerine pieces. Pour over frozen crust. Bake in preheated oven for 45 to 55 minutes or until the top is light brown and the center has a slight jiggle to it. Cool on a rack for 2 hours. Cover with plastic wrap and refrigerate for at least 6 hours before decorating or serving.

3. DECORATION: Spread whipped topping evenly over cake. Garnish with tangerine.

Light Citrus

CHEESECAKE

SERVES 10 TO 12

TIP
Freeze leftover zest for future uses.

VARIATION
You can use orange or lemon cookies instead of butter cookies in the crust for an added flavor.

Preheat oven to 325°F (160°C)
9-inch (23 cm) cheesecake pan, ungreased, or springform pan with 3-inch (7.5 cm) sides, greased (for other pan sizes, see page 10)

CRUST

1 ½ cups	butter cookie crumbs	375 mL
3 tbsp	margarine, melted	45 mL

FILLING

3	packages (each 8 oz/250 g) Neufchâtel cheese or light cream cheese, softened	3
1 cup	lower-fat sour cream	250 mL
1 cup	granulated sugar	250 mL
4	eggs	4
¼ cup	all-purpose flour	50 mL
1 tsp	lemon zest	5 mL
1 tsp	orange zest	5 mL
1 tbsp	fresh lemon juice	15 mL
1 tbsp	orange juice concentrate	15 mL
1 tsp	vanilla	5 mL

DECORATION

8 oz	lower-fat whipped topping	250 g
½ tsp	lemon zest	2 mL
½ tsp	orange zest	2 mL

1. CRUST: In a medium bowl, combine cookie crumbs and margarine. Press into bottom of cheesecake pan and freeze.

2. FILLING: In a large mixer bowl, beat cheese, sour cream and sugar on medium-high speed for 3 minutes. Add eggs, one at a time, beating after each addition. Mix in flour, lemon zest, orange zest, lemon juice, orange juice and vanilla. Pour batter over frozen crust. Bake in preheated oven for 45 to 55 minutes or until the top is light brown and the center has a slight jiggle to it. Cool on a rack for 2 hours. Cover with plastic wrap and refrigerate for at least 6 hours before decorating or serving.

3. DECORATION: In a medium bowl, combine whipped topping and zests. Spread evenly over cake.

Pumpkin Maple

CHEESECAKE

> Maple syrup adds a rich flavor accent to pumpkin that's worth the few more calories in each serving.

SERVES 10 TO 12

TIP
Pure maple syrup has much more flavor than typical pancake syrups.

Preheat oven to 325°F (160°C)
9-inch (23 cm) cheesecake pan, ungreased, or springform pan
with 3-inch (7.5 cm) sides, greased (for other pan sizes, see page 10)

CRUST

1½ cups	gingersnap cookie crumbs	375 mL
3 tbsp	margarine, melted	45 mL

FILLING

3	packages (each 8 oz/250 g) Neufchâtel cheese or light cream cheese, softened	3
1 cup	lower-fat sour cream	250 mL
1 cup	granulated sugar	250 mL
½ cup	pure maple syrup	125 mL
3	eggs	3
¼ cup	all-purpose flour	50 mL
¼ cup	pumpkin purée (not pie filling)	50 mL
2 tsp	vanilla	10 mL
1 tsp	ground cinnamon	5 mL
½ tsp	ground nutmeg	2 mL
¼ tsp	ground cloves	1 mL
¼ tsp	ground allspice	1 mL

DECORATION

8 oz	lower-fat whipped topping	250 g
½ tsp	ground cinnamon	2 mL

1. CRUST: In a medium bowl, combine gingersnaps and margarine. Press into bottom of cheesecake pan and freeze.

2. FILLING: In a large mixer bowl, beat cheese, sour cream and sugar on medium-high speed for 3 minutes. Add maple syrup in a steady stream while the mixer is going. Add eggs, one at a time, beating after each addition. Beat in flour, pumpkin, vanilla, cinnamon, nutmeg, cloves and allspice. Pour batter over frozen crust. Bake in preheated oven for 45 to 55 minutes or until the top is light brown and the center has a slight jiggle to it. Cool on a rack for 2 hours. Cover with plastic wrap and refrigerate for at least 6 hours before decorating or serving.

3. DECORATION: Spread whipped topping evenly over cake. Dust with a sprinkling of ground cinnamon.

Tropical

CHEESECAKE ❦

Island fruits are so naturally sweet you'll think you're eating a high-fat cheesecake.

❦

SERVES 10 TO 12

TIP
If papaya is not available, mangoes are
a good substitute.

VARIATION
Use ¼ cup (50 mL) drained juice from pineapple to flavor lower-fat whipped topping and ice cheesecake instead of garnishing with fruit.

Preheat oven to 325°F (160°C)
9-inch (23 cm) cheesecake pan, ungreased, or springform pan
with 3-inch (7.5 cm) sides, greased (for other pan sizes, see page 10)

CRUST

1½ cups	vanilla cookie crumbs	375 mL
3 tbsp	margarine, melted	45 mL

FILLING

4	packages (each 8 oz/250 g) Neufchâtel cheese or light cream cheese, softened	4
1½ cups	granulated sugar	375 mL
8 oz	egg replacement	250 g
¼ cup	all-purpose flour	50 mL
1	can (7.5 oz/227 g) crushed unsweetened pineapple, drained	1
½ cup	chopped papaya, about ½ medium	125 mL
2 tsp	vanilla	10 mL

DECORATION

1	can (8 oz/250 g) crushed unsweetened pineapple, drained	1
½ cup	chopped papaya, about ½ medium	125 mL

1. CRUST: In a medium bowl, combine cookie crumbs and margarine. Press into bottom of cheesecake pan and freeze.

2. FILLING: In a large mixer bowl, beat cheese and sugar on medium-high speed for 3 minutes. Add egg replacement in a steady stream while the mixer is going. Mix in flour. Fold in pineapple, papaya and vanilla. Pour batter over frozen crust. Bake in preheated oven for 45 to 55 minutes or until the top is light brown and the center has a slight jiggle to it. Cool on a rack for 2 hours. Cover with plastic wrap and refrigerate for at least 6 hours before decorating or serving.

3. DECORATION: Top cake with pineapple and papaya.

Sauces

Classic Whipped Cream

TOPPING

½ cup	whipping (35%) cream	125 mL
2 tbsp	granulated sugar	25 mL

A whipped cream topping never goes out of style. You can use this classic on almost any cheesecake in this book.

1. In a well-chilled bowl, whip cream on medium-high speed until soft peaks form. With the mixer still running, sprinkle sugar into cream and continue whipping until firm peaks form. Pipe a whipped cream ribbon around the cake or ice the entire cake with topping.

MAKES ABOUT
1 CUP (250 ML)

TIP
For perfect whipping results, see Whipping Technique (page 18).

Fresh Blackberry

SAUCE

Plump blackberries, fresh from the produce stand, make this a rich decadent sauce. I use leftovers on pancakes for brunch.

MAKES ABOUT 2 CUPS (500 ML)

TIP

Use a strawberry huller to remove the insides of the blackberries. Sometimes the hulls of the blackberries create a bitter taste.

2-quart (2 L) heavy saucepan

1 lb	fresh blackberries, cleaned and hulled (see Tip, left)	500 g
⅓ cup	granulated sugar	75 mL
1 tbsp	cornstarch	15 mL
2 tsp	cold water	10 mL
¼ tsp	almond or rum extract	1 mL

1. In a saucepan, heat blackberries and sugar on medium until they begin to boil, about 3 to 5 minutes.

2. In a small bowl, combine cornstarch and water. Pour into boiling berries. Reduce heat to low and stir with a whisk until berries start to thicken, about 2 to 4 minutes. Heat for an additional 2 minutes. Remove from heat and whisk in almond extract. Cool to room temperature before refrigerating. Sauce will keep in a covered container in refrigerator for up to 1 week.

Fresh Raspberry

SAUCE

This sauce is a staple in all pastry kitchens as well as my own. You can create many desserts with it. Fold into whipped cream for a mousse, use as a topping on ice cream or drizzle on warm chocolate brownies.

**MAKES ABOUT
2 CUPS (500 ML)**

TIP
You can use frozen berries that have been individually quick frozen and not packed in sugar syrup. Just make sure you thaw out the berries before using.

VARIATION
Omit the liqueur for a thicker sauce.

2-quart (2 L) saucepan

2½ cups	fresh raspberries	375 mL
½ cup	granulated sugar	125 mL
2 tbsp	cornstarch	25 mL
¼ cup	cold water	50 mL
2 tsp	fresh lemon juice	10 mL
¼ cup	raspberry liqueur	50 mL

1. In a saucepan, heat berries and sugar on medium heat, until they begin to boil, about 3 to 5 minutes.

2. Remove from heat and using a fine mesh strainer, strain seeds from the mixture. (You can keep the seeds in, if you desire.) Return juice to heat and bring to a boil.

3. Meanwhile, in a small bowl, blend cornstarch and cold water to make a milky substance. Pour into boiling juice and whisk to incorporate. Heat until berry juice is no longer cloudy, the color is ruby red and thickened. Remove from heat. Add raspberry liqueur and whisk to incorporate. Cool completely before storing in a covered container in the refrigerator for up to 1 week.

Fresh Strawberry

SAUCE

MAKES ABOUT
3 CUPS (750 ML)

VARIATION
You can ignite
the liqueur with
a match after you
have heated it.

10-inch (20 cm) skillet

¼ cup	unsalted butter	50 mL
½ cup	packed brown sugar	125 mL
4 cups	strawberries, halved	1 L
¼ cup	orange-flavored liqueur	50 mL

1. In a skillet, melt butter over high heat. Add sugar and cook, stirring, until melted, about 3 to 5 minutes. Add berries. (If using larger berries, cut into smaller pieces before cooking so they will cook faster.) Stir and cook until sugar is a brick red color, about 5 to 8 minutes. Remove from heat and carefully add liqueur. Serve warm or let cool. Sauce will keep in a covered container in refrigerator for up to 1 week.

Cherry Almond

You can use frozen cherries if fresh are not available. This sauce tastes great with the Brownie Cheese Pie (see recipe, page 131).

❧

**MAKES ABOUT
2 CUPS (500 ML)**

TIP
If using frozen cherries, try to purchase ones that have been individually quick frozen and not packed in juice. If the cherries are packed in juice, drain before using.

VARIATION
To create a creamy sauce, add ¼ cup (50 mL) warm whipping (35%) cream into the cooked cherries.

2-quart (2 L) heavy saucepan

¾ lb	cherries, pitted and drained if fresh, or thawed if frozen (see Tip, left)	375 g
¾ cup	granulated sugar	175 mL
1 tbsp	cornstarch	15 mL
2 tsp	cold water	10 mL
½ tsp	almond extract	2 mL

1. In a saucepan, heat cherries and sugar on medium until they begin to boil, about 3 to 5 minutes.

2. In a small bowl, combine cornstarch and water. Pour into boiling cherries. Reduce heat to low and stir with a whisk until cherries start to thicken, about 2 to 4 minutes. Heat for an additional 2 minutes. (If the cherries do not break up while cooking, you can use a potato masher to slightly smash the fruit.) Remove from heat and whisk in almond extract. Cool to room temperature before refrigerating. Sauce will keep in a covered container in refrigerator for up to 1 week.

Espresso Cream

SAUCE ❧

Pool this cream sauce on a plate prior to placing a cheesecake slice on top. Use it with any chocolate or coffee-flavored cheesecake.

❧

MAKES ABOUT
1½ CUPS (375 ML)

VARIATION
You can substitute orange or almond-flavored liqueur for the coffee-flavored liqueur.

2-quart (2 L) saucepan

1 cup	whipping (35%) cream	250 mL
¼ cup	granulated sugar	50 mL
¼ cup	brewed espresso	50 mL
2 tbsp	coffee-flavored liqueur	25 mL

1. In a saucepan, heat cream, sugar and espresso until bubbles form around the sides and sugar is dissolved, about 3 minutes. Remove from heat and stir in coffee-flavored liqueur. Use warm or cold.

2. This sauce will keep in the refrigerator, in a covered container for up to two weeks. Warm it up in the microwave for 1 minute on Medium for a heated sauce.

Orange Mist

GLAZE

After placing fresh strawberries on top of a cheesecake you can mist this glaze on top of the berries for a "wet look". I like to use a spray mister for this glaze. It will coat more evenly.

MAKES ABOUT
1½ CUPS (375 ML)

2-quart (2 L) saucepan

1 cup	granulated sugar	250 mL
¼ cup	water	50 mL
¼ cup	orange or rum liqueur	50 mL

1. In a saucepan, bring sugar and water to a rapid boil, about 5 to 8 minutes or until sugar is dissolved. The glaze will be syrupy and you will be able to spray it out of a mister bottle. Remove from heat and add liqueur.

2. Place into a spray mister bottle and mist on top of berries. (You can also mist cakes with this glaze prior to icing.) Glaze will keep in a covered container in refrigerator for up to 2 weeks.

Coffee-Flavored

SYRUP

This sauce is so fast and easy to make, but your guests will think you worked all day on it. Drizzle on top of the Chocolate Espresso Swirl Cheesecake (see recipe, page 70).

MAKES 1 CUP (250 ML)

VARIATION
Substitute almond liqueur for the coffee-flavored liqueur for a nutty taste.

2-quart (2 L) saucepan

½ cup	granulated sugar	125 mL
¼ cup	water	50 mL
¼ cup	coffee-flavored liqueur	50 mL

1. In a saucepan, bring sugar and water to a boil, about 5 to 8 minutes or until sugar is dissolved. (Make sure you heat sugar and water to a full boil and cook until sugar is dissolved or the sugar may crystallize.)

2. Remove from heat and add liqueur. Use this syrup warm or cooled drizzled on cheesecake. Syrup will keep in a covered container in refrigerator for up to 2 weeks.

Port Wine Berry

SAUCE

*S*uch an easy
sauce and so tasty
too! Serve on top
of the Tri-Berry
Cheesecake for an
added berry punch
(see recipe, page 51).

MAKES ABOUT
3 CUPS (750 ML)

TIP
To make superfine
sugar, place the
amount called for
into
a food processor and
process for 2 minutes.

1 ½ lbs	fresh berries, such as strawberries, raspberries, blackberries and/or blueberries	750 g
½ cup	superfine sugar (see Tip, left)	125 mL
¼ cup	aged port, optional	50 mL

1. Place berries in a large bowl. Pour sugar and port, if using, on top and toss. Let stand for 30 minutes to one day prior to use. Keep in the refrigerator until needed. The berry sauce will keep as long as the berries are fresh, for 1 to 4 days.

Island
FRUIT COMPOTE

This compote is a great topping for any of the lemon cheesecakes. If you have any leftover, you can use it on chicken breasts.

**MAKES ABOUT
3 CUPS (750 ML)**

TIP
To tell if a mango or papaya is fresh, hold in the palm of your hand and gently squeeze. It is ready to use if it feels soft like a tomato.

½ cup	mango, peeled, seeded and diced, about 1 medium	125 mL
1 cup	pineapple, peeled, cored and diced	250 mL
½ cup	papaya, peeled, seeded and diced, about 1 medium	125 mL
½ cup	sweetened flaked coconut	125 mL
1 cup	rum	250 mL

1. In a medium bowl, combine all ingredients. Toss to coat completely. Place in the refrigerator for at least 1 hour prior to use. Compote will keep in a covered container in the refrigerator for 1 week as long as the fruit is fresh.

Truffle Fudge
TOPPING

When you just
need a little more
chocolate in your
cheesecake, top your
cake with a layer of
this fudge topping.
*I use any leftovers
on ice cream.*

MAKES ABOUT
2½ CUPS (625 ML)

TIP
You can reheat the
icing and use it
as a poured glaze.

Chocolate can be
a bit warm when
incorporating it into
the butter. This will
cause the butter to
melt and create a
different texture.

2-quart (2 L) double boiler

12 oz	milk chocolate, chopped	375 g
6 oz	semi-sweet or bittersweet chocolate, chopped	175 g
1 cup plus 2 tbsp	unsalted butter, softened	275 mL

1. In the top of a double boiler over simmering (not boiling) water, melt milk and semi-sweet chocolates together. Stir until smooth. Cool until no longer warm to the touch.

2. In a mixer bowl with whip attachment, beat butter and cooled chocolate on medium speed until uniform in color, about 3 minutes. Place mixer bowl with the frosting into the refrigerator for 10 minutes to firm the frosting. Return frosting to the mixer and beat for 2 minutes longer or until fluffy. Spread a thin layer of icing over the top of the cheesecake. Place the remainder of the icing into a pastry bag fitted with a star tip and decorate with a shell border around the top edge and around the bottom where the cake meets the plate.

White Chocolate Macadamia Midnight

SAUCE

I named this sauce when I was working late one night. It was close to midnight and there was a full moon. You can use this sauce on top of a pound cake, as well.

MAKES ABOUT 2 CUPS (500 ML)

TIP
When purchasing white chocolate, look at the ingredients and purchase one with cocoa butter. Avoid palm kernel, cottonseed and tropical oils, which will give the sauce a coconut flavor.

VARIATION
Substitute hazelnuts or cashews for the macadamia nuts.

2-quart (2 L) double boiler

12 oz	white chocolate, chopped	375 g
1 cup	whipping (35%) cream	250 mL
½ cup	toasted macadamia nuts, chopped	125 mL

1. In the top of a double boiler, over hot (not boiling) water, melt chocolate and cream. Stir until well blended. (The steam will melt the white chocolate without the aid of the heat of the flame. Please do not use the microwave to melt white chocolate. It has a lower melting point then other chocolates and will burn easily.)

2. After the chocolate has melted, remove the top part of the double boiler and cool the chocolate mixture until luke-warm. Add toasted macadamia nuts. This sauce can be used hot or cold.

Spiked Cranberry

SAUCE

I first served this on the side of my turkey for Thanksgiving and then tried it on top of the Blood Orange Cheesecake (see recipe, page 82). I knew I had a winner.

MAKES ABOUT
2 CUPS (500 ML)

TIP
Fresh orange juice makes a substantial difference in the flavor.

VARIATION
Blood oranges are flavorful in this topping when they are in season.

2-quart (2 L) saucepan

1 cup	granulated sugar	250 mL
½ cup	water	125 mL
1 tbsp	orange zest	15 mL
¼ cup	orange juice	50 mL
12 oz	fresh cranberries, about 3 cups (750 mL)	375 g
¼ cup	orange-flavored liqueur	50 mL

1. In a saucepan, combine sugar and water and bring to a boil. Add orange zest and juice and cranberries. Return to boil, then reduce heat and boil gently for 10 minutes or until the cranberries thicken and break open. Remove from heat. Add orange liqueur. Serve warm or cool on top of cheesecake.

Sources

EQUIPMENT AND SERVICES

Adventures In Cooking
973-305-1114
www.adventuresincooking.com
Fine chocolates, cheeses, Magic Line Pans, Microplane® zester/grater and spatulas.

Calico Cake Decorating Shop
714-521-2761
Cake decorating supplies, spatulas, molds and Magic Line Pans.

Cuisinart
203-975-4600
800-726-0190
www.cuisinart.com
Food processors and blenders.

George Geary, CCP
www.georgegeary.com
Author's website, full of recipes, tips, culinary tour information and teaching locations.

Parrish's Cake Decorating Supplies
310-324-2253
800-736-8443 (US only)
Magic Line Baking Pans, cheesecake pans, off-set spatulas, cake decorating supplies.

Sur La Table
800-243-0852
www.surlatable.com
Chain has a catalog division, cooking schools and cookware shops throughout the United States.

The Baker's Catalog®
King Arthur Flour
www.kingarthurflour.com
800-827-6836
Full of ideas, recipes, chocolates and baking supplies.

INGREDIENTS

BERRIES

Driscoll's Berries
"The World's Finest Berries"
800-871-3333
www.driscolls.com
Berry recipes and product information.

CHOCOLATE

Adventures In Cooking
(see info above)

Bernard Callebaut
800-661-8367
www.bernardcallebaut.com
Fine Belgian chocolate. Retail stores throughout Canada and the U.S. (Operates under the trade name Chocolaterie Bernard C in the United States.)

Lindt
www.lindt.com
800-701-8489
Swiss chocolate. Shop-online and order catalogue.

The Baker's Catalog®
(see info above)

EXTRACTS

Charles H. Baldwin & Sons
413-232-7785
www.baldwinextracts.com
Pure extracts from anise to peppermint. They also have a fantastic maple table syrup.

SPICES

Penzey's Spices
414-679-7207
800-741-7787 (US only)
www.penzeys.com
A family-owned premium spice company. Check out their catalog and remember to get all three kinds of cinnamons, as well as vanilla sugar, vanillas and candied ginger. Retail stores in nine states, with more to come.

VANILLA BEANS

Nielsen-Massey Vanillas
847-578-1550
800-525-7873
www.nielsenmassey.com
Fine producer of quality vanillas. They use a cold water process to optimize the favors of the beans. Organic products available.

National Library of Canada Cataloguing in Publication

Geary, George
    125 best cheesecake recipes / George Geary.

Includes index.
ISBN 0-7788-0054-7

1. Cheesecake (Cookery)
I. Title.   II. Title: One hundred twenty-five best cheesecake recipes.

TX773.G42 2002   641.8'653   C2002-901846-3

Index